THE 2023 FLORIDA RETIREMENT HANDBOOK

RYAN ERISMAN

Inside the Bubble: Unauthorized Guide to Florida's Most Popular Retirement Community

If you are thinking about buying a home and moving to The Villages, this could be the most important book you'll ever read. The Villages is one of the most popular retirement communities in the world, but if you're looking to move here, you need to do your due diligence and research. I'm constantly updating this guide with the latest information, resulting in the most comprehensive guide to The Villages available anywhere.

Learn more at insidethebubble.net/book/

Pick the Right Place

A step-by-step process for figuring out the best location, community, and home for *you*. 52% of my readers say that one of their greatest fears about retirement is moving to the wrong place. That's second only to not having enough assets or income. Imagine if there was a book to walk you step-by-step through the process of figuring out where to retire, and guiding you through all the steps required to actually make it a reality. That would be great right? Well, such a book does exist and it's called Pick the Right Place.

Learn more at picktherightplace.com/book/

CONTENTS

AUTHOR'S NOTE

What a difference a year makes! In my Author's Note from last year's edition of this book I wrote about the unprecedented increase in demand (and with that, higher real estate prices) that Florida was experiencing, mostly due to the effects of the coronavirus pandemic.

This year, it's a different story.

The real estate market started 2022 hot. But by the time I'm writing this in November of 2022, the bidding wars and quickly rising prices have been replaced by an increase in homes on the market, and builders and home sellers offering an ever-growing list of offers and incentives to get people to buy those homes.

Of course that's not the case everywhere. There are still exceptions to the rule, such as communities like The Villages and Latitude Margaritaville where demand still outpaces the number of homes available. But for the most part I can report that the market has calmed down to what we would call "normal". Next year I'll tell you whether or not it stayed there!

Last year I wrote:

 "I've been at this for nearly two decades and I've seen a lot, so I can tell you with great confidence things will calm down eventually, I just can't say when exactly."

This year I can tell you that "when" is now. If you've previously put your Florida retirement plans on hold, discouraged by the rising prices of the last few years, 2023 just might be your year.

This book will hopefully help you make the most of it. Thank you for buying it and trusting in my advice. I'm excited for you and can't wait to help you get wherever it is you're going.

The best way to keep up with all of the changes to the Florida retirement landscape as the next year goes by is to **subscribe to my newsletter at floridaforboomers.com**.

If you're not already a subscriber, it's free, so just visit that website and you'll see links to sign-up for the newsletter.

Talk soon!

Ryan Erisman

SO, you're thinking of retiring to Florida or maybe buying a second home or vacation home here.

You won't exactly be blazing a new trail!

Though likely inhabited by Native Americans for thousands of years before Europeans set eyes on it, Florida was "discovered" in 1513 by Juan Ponce de Leon who claimed it for Spain. Ponce de Leon named it Florida, because he landed here during "Pascua Florida," the festival of flowers during the Easter season. The next several hundred years were a tumultuous time in Florida with various parts of the state changing hands several times between the Spanish, French, and British. After Britain's defeat in the Revolutionary War, Spain regained control of Florida, but later ceded it to the United States.

Florida became the 27th state on March 3, 1845.

Florida Fast Facts

Capital: Tallahassee

Nickname: The Sunshine State

State Flower: Orange Blossom

State Beverage: Orange Juice

State Bird: Mockingbird

State Tree: Sabal Palmetto Palm

Funky Fact: State Pie: Key Lime

Why Do People Move to Florida?

The two main reasons people consistently name for moving to Florida are the great weather, and the slower pace of life. But let me tell you about another attractive feature of living in Florida.

Low Taxes

Florida is consistently ranked among the states with the lowest tax rate. It has less than half the tax burden per capita as New Jersey, the nation's highest tax state per capita, making it a haven for retirees as well as businesses. The state sales tax is 6%. One thing that attracts many people to Florida is that there is no state income tax. Any income that you plan to pull in from investments, pensions, or a second career during your retirement will only be taxed at the federal rate, which means more money for you in the end.

Another advantage is that since January 1, 2007, Florida residents no longer have to file an intangibles tax return on their stocks, bonds, mutual funds, money market accounts and other investments.

Weather

Florida is well known for its beautiful weather, with plenty of sunshine most days of the year. Thousands of Northerners affectionately referred to as "snowbirds" flock to the state each winter to escape the frigid winter temperatures up north.

During the winter, temperatures average around the mid-fifties in the north part of the state, and the mid-sixties down south. You won't find coat closets in most of the homes you see in Florida, but don't let that fool you. In some parts of the state it can get below freezing, and it has even been known to snow.

Florida's weather is primarily subtropical, largely because it is nearly surrounded by water. In the summertime temperatures can get uncomfortably warm. Lots of folks who move to Florida from up north use the summer months to do some traveling, going back up north to see friends or traveling abroad.

This is something that you may want to consider as well. There are days, especially in South Florida, where the mercury can top 100 degrees.

The average temperature in North Florida during the summertime is around 80 degrees while the average in South Florida is in the low to mid-eighties. You can also usually count on an afternoon rain shower or thunderstorm to cool you off a little bit on most summer days. Be careful during those afternoon thunderstorms, as Central Florida is known as the lightning capital of the world. Florida has a rainy season that runs from June through October. This rainy season accounts for around 70% of Florida's annual rainfall, which is between 50 and 60 inches for most parts of the state.

In 2022 Hurricane Ian gave us a nasty reminder that the threat of hurricanes is very real, and I've devoted an entire chapter later in the book (Chapter 20) to hurricanes.

Other Fun Florida Facts

While you might know *some* of these basic Florida facts, I'm willing to bet there are more than a few here that may surprise you.

- Florida is the 22nd largest state in the country. It's 67 counties cover 65,755 square miles.
- Florida is the 3rd most populated state in the country, and it is the 8th most densely populated state.
- Florida is the southernmost state in the continental United States. The southernmost point in the continental U.S. is located in Key West.
- Florida was considered a British colony from 1763 through 1783.
- The highest point in Florida is Britton Hill in the Panhandle just south of the Florida-Alabama line. At 345 feet above sea level, this is the lowest high point of any state.
- Florida is home to 175 state parks, 37 state forests, 12 national parks or preserves, three national forests, and one national scenic trail.
- Florida has 1,197 miles of coastline and 825 miles of beautiful beaches.
- Florida is also home to more than 7,700 lakes, 11,000 miles of rivers, and more than 700 freshwater springs.
- The St. Johns River is the largest river in the state of Florida, and it is unique because it flows from south to north.
- Some endangered species that have protected habitats in Florida include bald eagles, West Indian manatees, Kemp's Ridley sea turtles, Florida panthers, humpback whales, Key deer, whooping cranes, and Gulf sturgeon.

- Florida has been hosting Major League Baseball teams for Spring Training for more than 100 years. There are currently 15 teams that make their Spring Training homes in Florida.
- Florida has 26 officially designated scenic highways.
- Pelican Island was the country's very first national wildlife refuge.
- Florida leads the entire nation in toll roads, bridges, and golf courses.
- Florida produces more tomatoes, strawberries, sugar, and watermelons than any other state.
- At a total size of 11.5 million acres, The Florida Everglades is the largest subtropical wilderness in the country.
- No matter where you are in Florida, you are never more than 60 miles from a beach.
- Seven of the world's 10 most-visited theme parks are located in Florida.
- Florida is known as the lightning capital of the United States.
- Florida also leads the nation in average precipitation.
- Florida has more than 9,200 miles of hiking, bicycling, and equestrian trails, as well as more than 4,000 miles of paddling trails.
- More than 900 fishing world records were set in Florida, which is more than any other state or country in the entire world.
- Brevard County, Florida uses the area code 3-2-1 as a tribute to the Kennedy Space Center countdowns.

- John Pennekamp Coral Reef State Park in Key Largo was the country's very first underwater state park.
- Bird watchers can track more than 516 species of birds across the state of Florida.
- Crystal River is the only place in North America where it is legal to swim with manatees.
- The Great Florida Birding Trail is a statewide network that includes an astounding 510 wildlife viewing sites that are perfect for bird watching.
- Florida Southern College in Lakeland boasts the country's largest collection of buildings by famous architect Frank Lloyd Wright.
- Florida hosted the first integrated professional baseball game in Daytona Beach. That game featured the legendary Jackie Robinson.
- Florida is the only state to have an embassy in Washington, D.C.
- In terms of square miles, Jacksonville is the largest city in the contiguous United States.
- The world's smallest police station is a phone booth in Carrabelle, Florida.
- Mechanical refrigeration was invented in Florida by Dr. John Gorrie back in 1851.
- The largest parade of golf carts took place in September 2005 in The Villages, FL with 3,321 carts participating. Residents tried to break their own record in 2010 but "only" 3,124 showed up that year.

- According to some estimates, there is more than 2 trillion dollars worth of lost treasure in all of the sunken ships within 60 miles off the coast of Florida. (If you find some I want a cut!)

Florida Informational Websites

When I wrote the first edition of this book, the state of Florida's official website, myflorida.com, was a great resource for answering questions like how to get a Florida driver's license, researching the history of Florida, and finding information about taxes, insurance, roadways, employment, recreation, or health care.

However, since that time myflorida.com has morphed into just a directory of state agencies and information about reaching the governor. Great if that's all you need, but not so great otherwise.

In recent years, I've found myself pointing people towards stateofflorida.com instead.

This website, while not affiliated with, owned by, operated by, endorsed by, or approved by the State of Florida, includes plenty of information that the before mentioned myflorida.com website *used* to provide, so you might want to check it out.

If you are looking for information about things to do in Florida, the best place to look is the state's official tourism marketing website, visitflorida.com.

I've also included several pages of additional Florida information and resources in the back of this book in a chapter titled "Florida Resources".

CHAPTER TWO
TYPES OF COMMUNITIES

AS YOU RESEARCH the various communities I mentioned in this book, you'll come across a few different types of communities, as well as a few different types of homes.

That's what we'll look at in this chapter and the next.

There are several kinds of Florida communities that you may come across in your search, and here I've detailed a few of the more popular types. Keep in mind that it's entirely possible to come across communities that are combinations of these, for example, a gated 55+ maintenance-free community.

Country Club Communities

Florida has more golf courses than any other state. There are more than 1,500 golf courses in Florida and most cities have several golf course communities, also referred to as Country club communities. Courses can range from fairly modest to extremely upscale. Florida even has a license plate proclaiming it as the "Golf Capital of the World."

Many communities have more than one golf course. Most have at least one clubhouse with such amenities as a fitness center, practice facilities, pro shop, restaurants and bars, banquet facilities, even full-service spas, so that you can enjoy a massage after that tough round of golf.

Some golf courses are private, meaning you must be a member or the guest of a member to play there. Membership rates vary among country clubs depending on the location and caliber of the course.

Keep in mind that most private courses have a food and beverage minimum, meaning that you have to spend at least "x" amount of dollars in their restaurants and bars within a designated period of time. Thankfully, sometimes purchases in the pro shop can be applied towards meeting your food and beverage minimum. If you lose as many golf balls as I do, you should have no problem reaching your food and beverage minimum.

Many country club communities have equity memberships, which pass from one party to another through the sale of real estate in that community. If this is the case with the home you intend to purchase, be sure that the real estate contract includes the right to the membership. Your real estate agent can help you with this.

Some communities have both a private course and a public course. You can own a home in a community such as this, not be a member and instead choose to play the public course exclusively. Surely, though, if your budget allows you will probably want to be a member of the private course to give your golf game some variety.

Country club communities with a golf course that is always open to the public are also an option. Be aware, however, that public courses tend to be more crowded than private courses, although this can depend on the time of year, the level of the course, and the price you have to pay to play. Some new communities allow the public to use their golf courses until there are enough residents and consequently enough members in the community. This is both good common sense and sound economics.

If you do not play golf, you may want to think twice about buying a home in a golf course community. Many people who do not play golf resent the fact that they are sometimes required to help fund its operations through their homeowners' association dues. Whether or not this occurs depends on how the homeowners' association and club budgets are set up, so you might want to look into that before you buy.

Active Adult / 55-Plus communities

55-plus communities are communities where the majority of the homeowners are over the age of 55. For a community to qualify for the 55-plus designation and to be marketed as such, at least 80 percent of the units have to be occupied by at least one person over 55. A common misconception is that everyone must be over 55 but that simply isn't true. On the other hand, this does not mean that someone under 55 must be allowed to purchase a home. A community-- through its deed restrictions-- can legally deny someone the ability to purchase a home if they are not yet 55 years old. Some 55-plus communities also have limits on how long relatives such as kids or grandkids can visit.

Maintenance-Free Lifestyle Communities

If cutting grass, landscaping, painting, pressure washing, and general upkeep of the exterior of your home are appealing to you, skip to the next section. Still with me? Okay then, a maintenance-free community might be for you. While some maintenance-free communities are designated 55 and better, many are not. But because maintenance-free lifestyle commu nities often have restrictions such as no fences, no swing sets, and no basketball hoops, they tend to discourage many families with young children from moving in.

So, in maintenance-free lifestyle communities you might enjoy a little more peace and quiet but at the same time be free to have your children or grandchildren visit how often and how long you like.

Maintenance-free communities are those in which you pay a monthly, quarterly, or yearly fee (sorry, the "free" in "maintenance-free" doesn't refer to the cost) to a homeowners' association or resident association, and in return, the association contracts with outside vendors to take care of certain maintenance and upkeep. Some homeowners' associations fees just include the cutting of your grass and leave the homeowner to take care of other items or contract with vendors directly to have them done. Others include complete landscaping such as shrub trimming, mulching, fertilizing and spraying of the yards, painting, and pressure washing.

Most maintenance-free communities are highly "amenticised", with clubhouses, swimming pools, billiard and card tables, craft rooms, fitness centers, and activity directors. The idea is that you fill your time doing the things you enjoy, while leaving the work to someone else.

Manufactured Home Communities

Most retirees entertaining the purchase of a manufactured home in Florida will be considering manufactured home communities that offer a full array of amenities like golf, tennis, swimming pools, clubhouses, and restaurants and bars. It's not just the home, it's the lifestyle that retirees are after, and many developers have realized this and are offering it to the manufactured home buyer.

However, in many (though not all) manufactured home communities in Florida, you do not own the land your home sits on, the developer does. One of the main factors in a home's ability to appreciate is its location and land value, something that in this arrangement you have almost no stake in. This is often times a thorn in the side of residents, but it is what it is. If you really want to live there, it's simply something you'll have to deal with.

Also, the developer will pay the taxes and provide the services outlined in the developer agreement such as grounds maintenance, lawn care, security, and the like, and in turn will charge you a fee, commonly referred to as "lot rent." This is a source of revenue for the developer. The developer is providing you certain services, and you are paying him for providing them. Likewise, when the developer has an increase in costs or taxes, these increases will be passed on to the homeowners.

One of the best ways to find out more about what owning and living in a manufactured home in Florida might be like is to talk with people who live in a manufactured home. If you are curious, when visiting an area spend some time driving around a manufactured home community and talk with some residents if possible. Most will be glad to share their experiences with you, whether they are good or bad.

For more information on Manufactured homes in Florida, visit the Florida Manufactured Housing Association at: fmha.org

Gated Communities

Just as in several other states, maybe even your own, gated communities are located all over Florida. Gated communities are gaining in popularity across the nation, especially in the Sunbelt. They can either be manned, with guards posted at the gates and patrolling the streets regularly, or they can be unmanned, with arms or gates that open when you press a button on your garage door opener or enter your secret code in a call box.

Guests will either be required to stop and speak to the guard or call your home from the call box before proceeding into the community. While this can sometimes be inconvenient for some people, there is no doubt that gated communities do a good job at keeping solicitors, sightseers, and general riffraff out of the neighborhood, as well as protecting and enhancing the value of the homes in a community.

If your home in Florida is just going to be a part time residence, you might enjoy the added peace of mind that a gated community can give you while you are away. Guards in some communities will even check your doors and windows for you while you are gone. Some can act as a sort of concierge service, accepting packages for you and putting them aside for you until you return. When considering a gated community, be sure to ask your salesperson or real estate agent what level of service you can expect from the guards in the community you are considering.

If you get a chance, speak to a guard and see if they can give you any tips either on the community or the area you are considering. Guards typically see hundreds of people every day and therefore have their fingers on the pulse of the community.

But do not let the fact that a community is gated lull you into a false sense of security. No community, gated or otherwise, is immune to crime. Crime can happen anywhere, it does not discriminate based on zip code. Remember to keep your doors locked, garage door closed, and store any valuables in a safe place.

CHAPTER THREE
TYPES OF HOMES

WHEN CONSIDERING a home purchase in Florida, or anywhere for that matter, one of the first decisions you should make is whether to have a home built or buy a resale (previously occupied) home. Your decision will depend on several factors including how quickly you need a home, your personal taste, and other factors. Here are some pros and cons of both.

Pros of Building a New Home

One of the best things about a brand new home is that it is under warranty from the builder. If (almost) anything goes wrong while the home is under warranty, you won't be charged to have it fixed.

Assuming you are building from scratch (not buying a builder spec home), you will get to choose your own décor like carpet, tile, cabinets and counters. This helps to personalize the home to your tastes and to give it some of your own soul. You also have the ability to customize to an extent, depending on what types of changes the builder allows.

Also, you will likely qualify for better insurance rates because the home will be built to current building codes.

Cons of Building a New Home

One of the cons of building a new home is that you typically have to wait for the home to be built, unless the builder has the style of home you want in his inventory (commonly referred to as "spec" homes or "quick move-in" homes). If you are on a tight schedule, or you do not want to find a temporary place to live while your home is under construction, you might want to pass on building a new home.

Another important factor to consider is that building a new home can be an overwhelming and nerve-wracking process. Seeing little day-to-day progress can be exasperating and many people feel the urge to micromanage the builder when there is usually no need to do that. If you are predisposed to being a micromanager, skip the headaches and buy a home that's already built.

Pros of Resale Homes

One advantage of buying a resale home is that unless you have plans to do some remodeling before you move in, the home is ready to be occupied, and you know exactly what you're getting. You get to avoid the roller coaster of emotions involved in building a new home.

Most home sellers are open to at least some negotiation on price. This depends on the market of course, and in some cases, why the seller is selling. Helping you negotiate is where your real estate agent comes in handy.

Cons of Resale Homes

With a resale home you are not able to choose your décor such as tile and carpet, cabinets and countertops, or make any customization or personalization until after the purchase and, even then, not without a remodeling budget. It is what it is. Someone else has chosen the colors and materials, and their tastes may differ from your own. Something else to consider is that, depending on the age and construction of the home, your insurance may cost more.

Additionally, if you want the protection of a home warranty, it must be purchased separately at your expense, unless the seller provides one. Also, don't forget you'll need a home inspection, which you can read more about in a later chapter.

Single-Family Homes

The most basic and most popular type of home is the single family home. It's what most people think of when someone says "house". A standalone structure, a single-family home sits on its own piece of land, be it the size of a credit card or several acres. Single-family homes offer their owners the most sense of space.

Even if your neighbor's home is only five feet away, as will be the case in some communities, you still have a feeling of separation and distance from them. When standing in your living room, you really can't tell if the neighbor's house is five feet or 50 feet away.

Single-family homes typically offer the most flexibility when you wish to make changes, such as adding an addition, changing the exterior color, or putting in a pool.

If you buy a single-family home in a subdivision governed by a Homeowners' Association (HOA), you will not have as much flexibility with what you can do to your home.

The Architecture Review Board or ARB must typically approve most changes, especially those affecting the exterior appearance of the home. However, the upside is that your neighbors will have to conform to the same standards when they wish to make changes. Be sure to read the HOA restrictions before purchasing to make sure they are rules you are willing to follow.

As an owner of a single-family home, you will be responsible for the home's maintenance. You will be responsible for cutting the grass, trimming the shrubs and bushes, painting, pressure cleaning, and any other exterior maintenance as needed.

For the retiree who has better things to do than to spend Saturday on yard work, however, the new trend in some communities in Florida is for single-family homes to be maintained on the outside, just like a townhouse or condo. These are called "maintenance-free communities" or "maintenance-free lifestyle communities." Just as in a townhouse or condo, the owner is assessed a fee to pay for certain services such as lawn care, periodic painting, and pressure washing.

Condominiums

Condominiums, or condos, are popular all over the state, but even more so in coastal areas. Condominiums are buildings comprised of several separate units. Theoretically, the price of the land that the condo is built on is spread across the units, with units on higher floors typically commanding higher prices and yielding better views.

For example, someone who wants to live on the ocean and may not be able to afford the several million-dollar price tags for a home may opt instead for a condo at a lower price. Even so, some condos run into the millions of dollars depending on location and features.

Condominiums are communities unto themselves. The beauty of condo living is that most of the upkeep of a regular single-family home is eliminated. There is no lawn to cut, no shrubs to trim, and you won't ever be asked to paint the building in your spare time on the weekend.

Amenities range from the bare bones with a swimming pool and fitness room, to total luxury with full-time concierge, doorman and valet, room service, spas, and restaurants.

I actually used to live in a condo on the ocean. There were things that I loved about condo living and things that I didn't like. Here are links to two articles I've written on the subject:

What I like about condo living:

floridaforboomers.com/what-i-like-about-oceanfront-condo-living/

What I don't like about condo living:

floridaforboomers.com/downsides-oceanfront-condo-living/

Townhouses and Attached Villas

Townhouses and Attached Villas can be considered sort of a happy medium between a single-family home and a condo.

Townhouses are typically two-story structures while attached villas are usually one-story structures. As opposed to condos, townhouses and attached villas are similar to single family homes in that they sit on their own piece of land.

They are also a little bit like a condominium in that they are attached to one or more other homes of similar size and style. They commonly include either a one or two-car garage and also a front or back patio for lounging outside.

The outside of the home is typically taken care of for you, you don't have anyone living directly above you, and there is frequently a small piece of the yard for you to call your own in which you can plant annuals or a rose bush, etc. (often subject to community restrictions).

This is what I like to call "lock and leave" convenience, and these benefits account for the rise in popularity of townhouse and attached villa living in Florida.

Like single family homeowners in most communities, townhouse and attached villa owners are assessed for the maintenance of the common areas (parts of the community owned equally by the home owners), as well as any amenities provided such as swimming pools, tennis courts, and pavilions. But they are also sometimes charged a little more than single family homeowners due to reserves for exterior painting and new roofing whenever it comes time for that.

These assessments can occur monthly, bi-monthly, quarterly or yearly. Most likely these fees will not be figured into your mortgage, so you will have to make a separate payment when it is due. Again, you should review the budget and the association rules before you make a purchase.

Manufactured Homes

Close your eyes and step into a modern manufactured home. Now open them. Are you sure that you're really in a manufactured home? You see drywall, crown molding, tile, hardwood floors, a fireplace, decorative niches, and archways. Then look at the floorplan and layout, it seems that this can't be a manufactured home!

Manufactured homes have come a long way from the long and narrow tin cans on wheels of the 50s, 60s, and 70s and have evolved into a logical, economical, and safe choice for many would-be homeowners. Affordability is one of the main factors driving the increase in manufactured home ownership.

Manufactured homes cost considerably less than their site-built counterparts, sometimes 25-50 percent less, in fact.

Money is one thing you say, but are they safe? Today's manu-factured homes are built in quality and environmentally controlled factories and adhere to current federal building codes. This, combined with the fact that they are anchored to the foundation on which they sit, a process that is overseen by local building inspectors, means a safe and secure home that can withstand the elements. Manufactured home builders' websites are often filled with testimonials of how their homes have been able to withstand hurricane force winds just as well and sometimes better than some site-built homes.

Before you jump in though, some caveats to consider: Though they may be built to withstand winds over 100 mph and are up to federal codes, manufactured homes are still feared by many insurers. It can be tough to find insurance on your manufactured home at a reasonable rate.

Also, when hurricanes threaten Florida, especially near the coast, manufactured home communities are almost always under mandatory evacuation orders, even if site-built home communities surrounding them are only under voluntary evacuation orders. That might be something to think about if you don't want to have to pick up and go every time the wind blows.

CHOOSING an area in which to live in Florida can be difficult, especially if you have not spent a lot of time here yet. There are many great choices available to you. But you can use these tips to narrow your choices down and eventually make a final decision on a place that fits your lifestyle and budget, suits your housing needs and desires, and that you'll love for years to come.

Getting Started

Since you likely live hundreds -- if not a thousand -- miles away from Florida, the best place to start your search is online. Visit the websites of the local newspapers for the cities, towns, or areas you are investigating and do some general exploring and reading.

You can often find information on the history of an area, photo tours and sometimes "virtual" video tours. It will also be helpful to read some local articles and editorials. These can give you a sense of the feel of an area and reveal items of interest or concern for the local residents.

Radio and TV news stations also have some excellent resources on their websites. Radio stations can be especially helpful for finding information in line with your interests.

For example, a community calendar for a country music station might list events that would appeal to their typical listener. These events would be different than events that might interest an oldies or easy listening crowd.

Next, visit the websites of the area chambers of commerce and request an information package if they have one available. The information packages will usually include a brochure on the area filled with advertisements for local businesses, information on annual events, a guide to local history, and more.

In addition, request information from some new home builders and communities in the area, to see if the types of houses they offer appeal to your wants and needs.

If the area seems like it might meet your requirements, go to the next step.

Links to most Chambers of Commerce can be found at: state-offlorida.com/chambers-of-commerce/

Getting Personal

It goes without saying that you should talk to friends or relatives living in Florida, but don't overlook people in your extended network or sphere of influence. For example, did your golf buddy's brother-in-law recently move to Florida? Give him a call and get the scoop!

Local Government

Visit the website of the local government. By the looks of things, are they up-to-date technologically? Read through official statements and press releases you may find. Does the local government seem prepared to manage the growth their area may be experiencing?

Also, what are the taxes like in the area? Is the government being wise and prudent in their spending, or does it seem like they are plundering windfalls from property tax increases? These are all not easily answered questions but with a little research you can get a feel for what some of the answers might be.

Home Prices

To get a general feel for what the prices of homes are in the area in which you are looking, visit sites like Realtor.com, Zillow.com, and Trulia.com. They will show you all the homes listed in the city or zip code that you specify. Enter your required number of bedrooms and bathrooms as well as your price range and see which homes come up as a result.

Florida Real Estate Shows

Florida real estate shows are a great opportunity to check out some of the new communities in Florida without even having to set foot in the state.

Home builders, developers, and real estate agents come to these shows in hopes of making a good first impression on potential buyers like you. The shows are set up so that you can wander around and stop for information at booths that look like they may be of interest to you.

Show locations are primarily in the Northeast and Midwest. The shows are typically in-person, but some moved online in 2020 and 2021 due to the pandemic.

One company that organize these shows is RPI Media. For more information on show dates and locations visit rpimedia.com.

Contact a Real Estate Agent

If you took the initiative to purchase and read this book, you know better than to simply trust that the first real estate agent who crosses your path will be able to adequately handle the complex details of your real estate purchase.

Unfortunately, this is not the case for many people.

According to the National Association of REALTORS®, 70 percent of people complete a real estate transaction with the first agent they made contact with.

In order to find the very best real estate agent for you, first ask friends or family who have moved to the area you are considering for referrals. If you don't have anyone to contact in the area you are considering, try doing an internet search, such as "Orlando real estate agent," and investigate the websites of several agents that come up.

It is a good idea to contact at least a few agents in the early stages to get a feel for what to expect down the road.

Ask the agents questions about their qualifications, years of experience in their market, and whether they have helped other people, particularly retirees like you, relocate to their area. They should be able to offer you written testimonials from satisfied clients.

Also, since you will be new to the area, make sure any real estate agent you choose to work with has a strong network of local service providers such as attorneys, home inspectors, and lenders to recommend to you.

Make a Visit

Now that you've gathered a bunch of information on places you think might interest you, it's time to make a visit.

When you visit an area, especially one you've never been to before, there are certain things you'll want to look for to help you decide if this is an area you might like to live in. Drive through some different parts of the local area, and as you are driving, keep in mind as to whether or not you are seeing restaurants, businesses, shopping centers and so forth that look appealing to you and that match your ideal lifestyle.

Stop in at some different establishments like restaurants or shopping malls and take a look around. Ask people you come in contact with what they like or don't like about the area.

See if they have any recommendations of places to look for homes or any other relevant information they are willing to share.

Drive Through Some Neighborhoods

Take a detour off the main roads and into some residential neighborhoods. Are the homes what you expected? Are people's yards well maintained?

Visit some of the new communities and model homes in the area or take a tour of some resale homes that you've arranged to see ahead of time with your real estate agent.

Facilities and Services

Look for the amenities that are important to you. Are there libraries nearby and are they up to date? What about medical facilities? Check to make sure an area's cultural activities, recreation facilities, beaches and parks, golf courses, and whatever else is important to you are available at a level that will fit your needs and desires.

Make a list of your current weekly activities (garden club, rotary, church, etc.) and be sure that the area you choose provides you the opportunities to continue to do what you enjoy.

You've Got Visitors!

Keep in mind the likes and dislikes of friends and family members who will be coming to visit. Do your kids and grandkids love the beach, or is a ten minute drive to Disney World more important? Presumably you will want them to visit as often as possible, so get their input before deciding on a place.

One of the worst things that could happen to you during this transition to life in Florida is you find your dream home but hate to go out into the community surrounding it for lack of things to do and be a part of.

Or you buy your dream home but find that when the kids and grandkids come to visit there's nothing fun for them to do.

But this won't happen to you as long as you do some prudent research and investigating before you make a purchase and settle in.

One other important thing to keep in mind is that some 55+ communities place a limit on the length of time that someone under the age of 19 years old can stay with you. In some communities this limit is as short as 30 days, so if you plan on hosting your grandkids for the entire summer, you better choose your community wisely.

Recently I was in the office of a sales manager for one of the top home builders in the country and he told me the story of one of his recent customers who moved to his community because the first community he moved to wouldn't let his grandkids visit for as long as he wished, so keep that in mind.

IN THE NEXT FEW CHAPTERS, I'll briefly discuss the major regions of Florida, and take a closer look at some of the most popular retirement cities within each region.

I'll also tell you about some new communities that are currently being developed in each region.

As you might imagine, new communities are popping up in Florida all the time, while other communities reach completion and are sold out.

On my website I do my best to maintain a current list of all the 55+ communities in Florida that are still selling new homes. You can access that list here:

floridaforboomers.com/list/

But how do you determine which one is right for you?

Location > Community > Home

Some readers come to me with their ideal house in mind, but they haven't really put much thought into where or in what kind of community they want that house to be in.

Your house is important, to be sure, but the location and type of community your home is in will mean so much more to you in retirement.

If I can impress one thing upon you with this book it is this:

> Think about your search in terms of location, then community, and then home.

Once you find an area you think you might like, check out the communities in that area. Once you find a community you could see yourself living in, then go on to explore the homes they offer.

In my experience this will result in a lot less frustration and increase your odds of picking the right place for you.

I discuss this concept in much more depth in my other book Pick the Right Place. Learn more at: picktherightplace.com/book/.

Non-Age Restricted Communities

While this book is primarily focused on active adult and age-restricted communities, I know that not everyone is looking for that, so I also maintain a list of notable Florida communities that **do not** have age restrictions.

You can see that list at:

floridaforboomers.com/all-ages/

Home Prices

Please keep in mind that home prices are subject to change without notice. I visited the websites of each community listed in this book in November 2022 and if pricing was available, I've listed it in the following pages. You'll find links to the websites for every community where you can find their most current pricing.

Don't get discouraged if the communities listed here in the places you are interested in have prices that are higher than you want to spend. In almost every place mentioned you can find slightly older homes in slightly older communities selling for less than their new home counterparts. This is where research on sites like Zillow.com and connecting with a local real estate agent like I discussed in the previous chapter will come in handy.

A Word About Advertising

I've done my best to include *every* 55+ community currently selling new site-built homes in Florida in the following chapters. While I do accept advertising on my website, **no communities have paid to be in this book**. In fact, the majority of them probably don't even know they're in this book, or that I or my website exist!

Some reviewers of previous editions of this book seemed to think this was a list of my favorite communities or communities that paid to be included, so I wanted to put that thought to rest.

CHAPTER SIX
FLORIDA PANHANDLE

THIS REGION IS home to the state's capital, Tallahassee, as well as Pensacola, Fort Walton Beach, and Panama City. People love the tranquility of the Panhandle, as it is one of the least heavily developed parts of Florida. However, as more people discover this region, this tranquility may not last.

Panama City Beach

Despite being a completely separate municipality, it is easy to confuse the history of Panama City Beach with the larger Panama City located just inland from Panama City Beach. However, these two entities offer very distinct opportunities.

Known for its 27-mile stretch of stunning white sand beaches, Panama City Beach is one of the most popular tourist destinations located in the Florida panhandle, and it's hard not to fall in love with what the city refers to as "The World's Most Beautiful Beaches." Tourists and residents alike are able to enjoy scenic state parks, exciting theme parks, and more golf courses than most can keep track of.

Originally discovered by Spanish explorers, the area that would become Panama City Beach was purchased by the United States in 1819. It then became a favorite location of General Andrew Jackson when he marched his troops through the Florida panhandle on their way to New Orleans. When the territory became available to settlers, many of Jackson's troops were the first to call Panama City Beach home.

Fast forward quite a few years and we will see that the early 2000's was one of the most interesting times in the history of Panama City Beach. This is when the real estate boom motivated builders and investors to upgrade many of the older beachfront buildings into modern condominiums and fabulous luxury homes. The area saw real estate values quadruple before coming back to earth after the real estate collapse in 2008.

The lifestyle in Panama City Beach starts and ends with that absolutely stunning 27-mile stretch of gorgeous white sand beaches. Whether you like to enjoy the beach by spending the entire day laying out in the sun or you prefer to walk for miles in the sugary sand, this is paradise for anyone who loves the beachfront lifestyle.

One of the most popular beach destinations in Panama City Beach is St. Andrews State Park, where visitors will find the perfect combination of beachfront beauty and natural surroundings. In addition to offering beach access, St.

Andrews State Park also picnicking and boating facilities, as well as two nature trails that are great for bird watching.

Destin

Destin Florida at Sunrise

Commonly referred to as "The World's Luckiest Fishing Village," Destin is located on a small peninsula along the Florida panhandle about halfway between Panama City and Pensacola. This area of Florida is known as the Emerald Coast because of the crystal clear green water of the Gulf of Mexico.

In addition to its beautiful waters, Destin is also known for its stunning white sand beaches. And as a popular tourist destination, there are a nearly unlimited number of things to do when it comes to attractions, golfing, shopping, and dining. The luckiest fishing village in the world is also known for... you guessed it...outstanding fishing.

Destin was named after Leonard Destin, who was a fisherman that settled here sometime between 1845 and 1850. The Destin area began to see rapid population growth in the early 1980s after condominiums began popping up in the 1970s.

Because of its reputation as a tourist destination, there is pretty much always something to do here in Destin. The area features really outstanding golf courses, and there are more than 40 different companies that offer fishing charters. Between all of those activities, you could spend years fishing and golfing right here in Destin without ever getting bored.

Keeping with the tourist-focused theme, another one of the most popular activities in Destin is kicking back and relaxing on one of the beautiful, powdery white sand beaches.

If you are looking for a bit of history or culture, you should definitely check out the Destin History & Fishing Museum or take in a performance at The Funky Blues Shack.

The Destin area offers the ideal small town beachfront community setting that is absolutely perfect for anyone who is passionate about fishing, golfing, or just relaxing on the beach. If you are looking for a retirement destination where every day feels like a vacation, Destin is a great place to start.

Pensacola

Located at the very far end of the panhandle, Pensacola is a perfect location for anyone looking to enjoy Florida's perfect weather and those beautiful Gulf Coast beaches, without relocating to one of the popular tourist destinations.

Between the outstanding fishing opportunities, the adventure of canoeing along the Blackwater River, and the history of the National Museum of Naval Aviation, there is a never-ending supply of activities to keep residents busy here.

This area holds a significant place in United States military history. Pensacola was the location for the very first US Naval Air Station, which was commissioned in 1914. Famous astronauts John Glenn and Neil Armstrong were trained here, and it is also home to the world-famous Blue Angels.

Like many cities along the Gulf Coast, the Pensacola lifestyle revolves around making use of its gorgeous white-sand beaches and exploring all of the nearby parks and nature preserves.

The beaches at Santa Rosa Island, Perdido Key State Park, the Pensacola Beach Gulf Pier, and the Gulf Islands are all popular choices. One of the favorite inland destinations is Blackwater River State Park. If you are into canoeing or kayaking, this is a perfect place to start exploring the local waterways.

Since the area has such a rich military history, the Pensacola lifestyle also includes a large number of museums and historic landmarks. Visitors should absolutely make a point to check out the National Naval Aviation Museum, the Pensacola Naval Air Station, the Pensacola Lighthouse and Museum, and historic Fort Barrancas.

Residents looking to appreciate the arts can usually find excellent options at the Saenger Theatre, the Pensacola Little Theatre, or the Pensacola Opera.

Pensacola Beach and Perdido Key is where you will find everything you need for a day at the beach. With lots of stores selling everything from swimwear and beach accessories to suntan lotion and souvenirs, this is the place to get your beach shopping on!

Between the rich history, the beautiful beaches, and all of the great shopping and dining options, there isn't much more you could want out of life here in Pensacola.

PANHANDLE AREA COMMUNITIES

Note: On my website I've got a handy list of all the communities mentioned in this book at:
floridaforboomers.com/list

Latitude Margaritaville – Watersound, FL

Latitude Margaritaville Watersound is a Jimmy Buffett-style community that is located about halfway between Panama City Beach and Miramar Beach. In addition to all of the standard Margaritaville amenities, residents here also enjoy access to their own private beach along Florida's Gulf Coast.

The list of amenities coming to Latitude Margaritaville Watersound is very similar to what we've seen in other Latitude Margaritaville communities.

The smallest homes at Latitude Margaritaville Watersound are called Cottages (Conch Collection) that range in size from 1,204 a/c sq. ft. to 1,466 a/c sq. ft.

The next size up are Villas (Caribbean Collection) that range in size from 1,503 a/c sq. ft. to 1,862 a/c sq. ft. After that there are two different collections of Single-Family Homes which max out at around 2,500 sq. ft. Prices start in the $300k's.

latitudemargaritaville.com/watersound

THE AREAS OF JACKSONVILLE, St. Augustine, and Palm Coast are where the bulk of the population in this fast-growing region live. Palm Coast is located in what was for a few years the nation's fastest growing county, Flagler County.

Jacksonville

Located right on the Atlantic Coast in northeast Florida, Jacksonville offers its residents all of the amenities that come with a beachfront city for a fraction of the cost of some of the popular destinations nearby.

Known as the "River City on the Sea," Jacksonville is packed with more than 22 miles of beaches, a scenic stretch of the beautiful St. Johns River, the largest urban park system in the nation, historic neighborhoods, and a thriving street art scene.

The history of Jacksonville dates all the way back to 2500 BC according to pottery remains that have been found in the area, but the modern history of the city starts when it was founded in the early 1800s. American settlers moving to the area named it after President Andrew Jackson.

Following the Civil War, Jacksonville became a popular winter tourist destination for wealthy visitors from the north. Then the real boom came to the area shortly after World War II thanks to the postwar economic growth that helped many cities in Florida become popular places to live.

In a city that is known for its beaches, waterways, and green spaces, everything about the lifestyle in Jacksonville revolves around taking advantage of those amenities.

Whether you are a surfer, an ocean swimmer, or just a beach bum, you can find your fill of salt water, sand, and sun at Jacksonville Beach, Neptune Beach, and Atlantic Beach.

In addition to those beaches, residents can also find tons of boating, fishing, and kayaking opportunities along the St. John's River, which is one of the few northward flowing rivers in the country.

If you prefer to stay on dry land, there are more than a few green spaces to choose from here in "The City of Parks," including 10 different state and national parks inside the city limits.

Where many Florida cities have cultural communities that you have to go looking for, you simply can't avoid all of the arts and culture that exists in Jacksonville. The Art in Public Places Program, which displays the city's art collection in public buildings, plays a major role in creating that atmosphere.

There are also more than 18 different museums and art galleries across the city that create a never-ending cycle of cultural excitement for anyone who is interesting in the arts.

And that's not even scratching the surface of all that Jacksonville offers through its thriving theatre community and all of the history that you will find in its unique neighborhoods.

Amelia Island (including Fernandina Beach)

The Palace Saloon is the oldest bar in Florida

People who make their homes on Amelia Island have been quoted saying things like, "It's the kind of place that captures your soul." They describe the area as "the type of place you feel like you spent your whole life searching for."

That may seem a bit over-the-top, but once you experience Fernandina Beach and Amelia Island for yourself, you will see that those residents are not exaggerating at all.

Located in the far northeast corner of the state, just north of Jacksonville, Amelia Island is stunningly beautiful and filled with history, culture, great shopping, championship level golf, world-class resorts, and a collection of incredible restaurants. That is a pretty impressive list when you consider that the island is only 13 miles long and two miles wide!

The history of Amelia Island contains a number of interesting twists and turns that involve the eight different countries that have controlled the island, the Civil War Fort located on the island, and of course its history of local pirates.

One of the most popular attractions on the island is Fort Clinch State Park. This park contains what remains of Fort Clinch, which is one of the most well-preserved American forts from the 19th century. Visitors will regularly find Civil War reenactments happening here, but the park is also a great place for beach activities!

As for cultural activities, you can catch regular shows at the Amelia Community Theatre and the Fernandina Little Theatre. There is also the Amelia Arts Academy, which is one of only four certified arts schools in Florida.

Fernandina Beach contains a historic downtown district that is filled with tons of culture, as well as excellent boutique shopping. On the second Saturday of every month, the downtown art galleries host "Artrageous Artwalks" where visitors can tour all of the local galleries and meet local artists.

For an island this small, there are an impressive number of golf course communities spread across Amelia Island.

Places that combine history, culture, and golfing with great weather and world-class dining can be found throughout Florida.

However, the manner in which those things come together in Fernandina Beach and Amelia Island makes this one place that you truly have to experience first-hand in order to appreciate. After spending some time on Amelia Island, most people don't ever want to leave!

St. Augustine

Famous for being the oldest city in the country, St. Augustine is absolutely the perfect place for anyone who appreciates history. The city is located along the east coast of Florida just about 45 minutes south of Jacksonville, and a little over an hour north of Daytona Beach.

In addition to being a great location for history buffs, St. Augustine is also filled with lots of culture, great shopping, and unique places to eat. If you are passionate about any combination of those things, the Nation's Oldest City could be a great option for your retirement!

St. Augustine was discovered by Spanish explorers all the way back in 1565. From that point, it served as the Spanish capital of "La Florida" for more than 200 years. The famous Spanish explorer Ponce de Leon believed to have found the fountain of youth here.

In the late 1700s, the territory of Florida came under British control. It was then transferred back to Spanish control shortly after and then eventually awarded to the United States in 1819.

Henry Flagler played a key role in the development of St. Augustine into a popular winter retreat for wealthy northerners. In his role as a partner with John D. Rockefeller, Flagler had tremendous connections and did a good deal to develop St. Augustine into the city it is today.

Today, the city still pays tribute to its rich history with an impressive collection of museums and historic buildings that are still standing.

With a history as rich as you'll find in St. Augustine, it should come as no surprise that there is also a thriving cultural community here as well. In addition to the many museums and historical monuments you will find throughout the city, there are also a number of cultural events and theaters that have their own historical significance.

You could spend entire days getting lost in the Lightner Museum, the Art Galleries of Saint Augustine, and the Butterfield Garage Art Gallery. There are also plenty of opportunities to take in performances at historic venues like the St. Augustine Amphitheater and the Limelight Theatre.

St. Augustine is also home to the St. Augustine Music Festival that celebrates classical music here every summer. In addition to all of the culture and history that St. Augustine is known for, there are also plenty of outdoor activities available for anyone seeking a more active lifestyle.

Many of the old historic monuments like Castillo de San Marcos, Mission of Nombre de Dios, and Fort Matanzas National Monument provide plenty of walking as you explore, which is great for everyone who is counting their steps these days.

And if you are looking for a really serious challenge, the 249 steps to the top of the St. Augustine Lighthouse are another great combination of history and exercise that are sure to get you another badge on your favorite step counter!

If you are passionate about wildlife, the St. Augustine Wild Preserve and Anastasia State Park are great places to see everything from alligators and otters to all of the local birds.

Everything about St. Augustine revolves around the fact that it is the oldest city in the country. But that doesn't mean you won't find modern amenities here. This community offers the perfect hybrid that brings the new and the old together in a way that celebrates its history without being stuck in it.

Whether you are a sucker for historic landmarks, enjoy the culture of a historic theatre, would like to get out and explore historic parks, or just want something good to eat, you can do it all in St. Augustine.

Palm Coast

Located along the Atlantic Coast about halfway between St. Augustine and Daytona Beach, Palm Coast offers the perfect combination of nature and golf for anyone who likes to enjoy both at the same time.

In a state where everything seems like a historic landmark, Palm Coast is actually a very new development. The city was just incorporated in 1999, so everything here is relatively new.

The area first started to be developed in 1969 when the ITT Community Development Corporation put together a plan for a community of 48,000 homes. Over the years, the area has grown by leaps and bounds and found its niche as a popular golf and tourist destination.

The Palm Coast Lifestyle definitely revolves around golf and nature, and even provides some opportunities for the two to intersect.

On the golf side, there are courses like the Ocean Course at Hammock Beach that allow you to play right along the Atlantic Ocean. Other popular courses include Palm Harbor Golf Course, The Grand Club Cypress Knoll Golf Course designed by Gary Player, and The Grand Club Pine Lakes Golf Course designed by Arnold Palmer.

If nature is more appealing to you, there are options like Washington Oaks Gardens State Park, Waterfront Park, Princess Palace Preserve, and many other local parks and preserves to explore.

Palm Coast is located less than an hour away from both St. Augustine and Daytona Beach, where you will find tons of theaters, museums, and galleries.

If you are passionate about either golfing or nature, Palm Coast is definitely a place you are going to want to consider when looking for a Florida retirement destination. But if you are passionate about both, it might be the only place you need to look!

NORTHEAST FLORIDA COMMUNITIES

Note: On my website I've got a handy list of all the communities mentioned in this book at: floridaforboomers.com/list

Del Webb Nocatee – Pontc Vedra, FL

Del Webb Nocatee is a 55+ gated community in Ponte Vedra, which is in Northeast Florida, just minutes from Jacksonville and St. Augustine, and about 4 miles from pristine beaches.

The Canopy Club will offer luxury amenities just a golf cart's drive away, including a zero-entry pool, pickleball courts, fitness studio, and even an onsite Tavern & Grill with private wine lockers. Prices start in the $400k's.

delwebb.com/homes/florida/jacksonville/ponte-vedra/del-webb-nocatee-210299

Del Webb eTown – Jacksonville, FL

Del Webb eTown is a community of 346 single-family homes in Jacksonville that began construction in 2018. Plans here call for over five acres of amenities that include an 8,000 square foot clubhouse and a resort-style pool. Prices start in the $400k's.

delwebb.com/homes/florida/jacksonville/jacksonville/del-webb-etown-210300

Del Webb Wildlight - Amelia Island Area

Del Webb Wildlight is a new 55+ community that recently opened north of Jacksonville in the Fernandina Beach/Amelia Island area. For those who plan to travel frequently, the community is only about 15 minutes from Jacksonville International Airport. You can expect to see the same types of homes and amenities offered in other Del Webb communities here in Florida. Prices start in the $300k's.

delwebb.com/homes/florida/jacksonville/wildlight/del-webb-wildlight-210713

Everlake at Mandarin - Jacksonville

Everlake at Mandarin offers 192 luxury paired villa homes centrally located in the heart of Mandarin, a popular Jacksonville area neighborhood. Residences will offer lakefront, preserve and privacy-focused homesites. The paired villas of Everlake are designed to liberate homeowners from day-to-day home maintenance so they have more time to pursue a carefree lifestyle.

Amenities will include a private clubhouse with an outdoor swimming pool, open-air pavilions, fitness center, and more.

Prices start in the $300k's.

dreamfindersactiveadult.com/everlake/

Lakeview at Tributary - Yulee, FL

Lakeview at Tributary is the 55+ section of the Tributary masterplan community. Residents can enjoy resort style amenities including a central lake, massive clubhouse with a pool, miles of nature trails and more.

Homes range in size from about 1,500 to 2,200 sq. ft. and start in the $300k's.

tributaryliving.com/lakeview-55-plus/

Matanzas Lakes – Palm Coast, FL

Matanzas Lakes is an age restricted community in Palm Coast with just over 100 homes. The community features two lakes, a zero-entry community pool/amenities center, gated entrances, and low-maintenance living for those at least 55 years of age.

Lawn care is included in HOA fees and there are no CDD fees. There are 7 different floorplans available ranging in size from 1,623 to 2,033 sq. ft. of living space. Prices start in the $300k's.

seagatehomes.com/find-your-home/matanzas-lakes/matan-zas-lakes

Parkland Preserve at World Golf Village - St. Augustine, FL

Located in historic St. Augustine, Parkland Preserve is a community of single-family homes that started construction in 2019. Community amenities include a swimming pool, fitness room, covered pavilion, park, and lifestyle director.

Parkland Preserve offers four different single-family floor-plans and prices start in the $300k's. At one point I heard there might be some condos going in there as well, but at the time of this writing there's nothing to indicate that on their website.

drhorton.com/florida/north-florida/st-augustine/parkland-preserve

Reverie at Trailmark - St. Augustine

Reverie at Trailmark is a 55+ community in St. Augustine. The Lodge is a 4,600 sq. ft. Lakeside Clubhouse that features indoor and outdoor social spaces, six pickleball courts, a resort-style pool and spa, catering kitchen, and what sounds to me like one of the coolest amenities...an open-air bier garten.

There are 11 new single-family home designs, ranging from 1,500 to 3,000 sq. ft. The community features lakeside and preserve homesites. Prices start in the $300k's.

dreamfindersactiveadult.com/trailmark/

Stillwater - St. Johns

Stillwater is a 55+ community located just off I-95 about 25 minutes south of downtown Jacksonville. Homeowners have access to exciting amenities, such as the Bobby Weed designed 18-hole golf course and a community swimming pool. Plus, there are plenty of restaurants and shops nearby in St. Johns.

A total of 549 homes are planned here and attached villages and single-family homes are available. Prices start in the $300k's.

lennar.com/new-homes/florida/jacksonville-st-augustine/st-johns/stillwater

Summer Bay at Grand Oaks - St. Augustine

Located in St. Johns County, this community from Pulte Active Adult features homesites designed to showcase conservation, lake and park views. The gated, 55+ neighborhood will have 1.5 acres of exclusive amenities including pickleball, tennis, bocce ball courts and more. Prices start in the $300k's.

pulte.com/homes/florida/jacksonville/st-augustine/summer-bay-at-grand-oaks-210797

Watersong at RiverTown – St. John's, FL

Located in master-planned community of RiverTown, Watersong at RiverTown is an active adult community of 800 attached villas and single-family homes. Residents here enjoy access to their own private community clubhouse, resort-style pool, and fishing pier.

Homes range in size from 1,431 to 2,554 square feet with 2 to 4 bedrooms and 2-3 bathrooms. Prices start in the $300k's.

watersongfl.com

CHAPTER EIGHT
CENTRAL EAST COAST

KNOWN AS THE "SPACE COAST" because of the Kennedy Space Center in Cape Canaveral, this region includes Ormond Beach, Daytona Beach, Port Orange, New Smyrna, Titusville, Melbourne, and Cocoa Beach. This region is growing rapidly not only because of Northerners retiring there, but also because of people moving up from South Florida, to escape the high home prices and congestion.

Ormond Beach

The city of Ormond Beach is best known for being located just north of the much larger, much busier Daytona Beach. However, there is quite a bit more to Ormond Beach and simply being "Daytona Beach Light".

The community contains a perfect mixture of modern art and culture, storied history, untouched nature and wildlife, championship golf, and some of the best small-town shopping and dining you will find anywhere!

The Ormond Beach area was original settled in the mid-1600s by Quakers who were headed for New England but ended up in Florida. After the local Timacuan Indians destroyed most of the original Quaker settlement in the early 1700s, the area was then settled by the Spanish and sea caption James Ormond.

Like its neighbor, Daytona Beach, the city of Ormond Beach has a rich history of automobile racing and has long been a favorite winter home for many famous residents, the most significant being John D. Rockefeller.

One of the most popular historic and cultural attractions in the Ormond Beach area is The Casements, which was the former winter home of John D. Rockefeller. Known as "The Jewel of Ormond Beach," The Casements was purchased by Rockefeller in 1918. After multiple other owners, the building eventually deteriorated and was left vacant until it was purchased by the city in 1973 and restored by The Casements Guild.

Other cultural venues in Ormond Beach include the Ormond Memorial Art Museum & Gardens and the Ormond Beach Performing Arts Center. The Ormond Memorial Art Museum & Gardens is known for displaying the work of many outstanding local artists, and the 600-seat Ormond Beach Performing Arts Center hosts all types of local cultural events.

While the local history and culture are great, one of the best things that Ormond Beach has to offer is the way that it combines modern amenities with the raw natural beauty of the Atlantic Coast. The city is located near dozens of state parks, community parks, and local waterways that all make for great places to relax and observe the local wildlife.

"The Loop" is a famous stretch of roadway that extends about 15 miles north of Ormond Beach and then circles back around to the city. Along this path of more than 30 miles you will find stunning views of the Atlantic Ocean, Tomoka State Park, Bulow Creek State Park, and a number of other local attractions.

With all of the local parks and natural waterways in the areas surrounding Ormond Beach, canoe and kayak trips are extremely popular among local nature-lovers. There are local tour guides that will take you on canoe or kayak trips along the Tomoka River State Canoe Trial or along Pelilicer Creek in Faver-Dykes State Park. There are also tours that combine kayaking and fishing enabling residents to get the most out of their local waterways!

When considering retirement options around Florida, many different areas offer similar amenities with some more focused in specific areas than others. Part of the appeal of Ormond Beach is that this community offers just about everything you could possibly want without the hustle and bustle that typically comes with that many options. This is truly a small-town beach community that just happens to offer big city amenities!

Daytona Beach

Beach driving is permitted on large parts of
Daytona Beach

Because of its popularity among race fans, motorcycle enthusiasts, spring breakers, and summer vacationers, Daytona
Beach is often overlooked by many retirees as they search for
a Florida retirement destination that will fit their ideal lifestyle. However, those popular reasons for visiting Daytona
Beach are really just scratching the surface of what residents
enjoy here throughout the year.

Located just over an hour northeast of Orlando, this oceanfront destination provides residents with everything they
could want from a big city on the beach.

The area that would become Daytona Beach was originally
settled as a citrus and sugar cane plantation by Samuel
Williams. That plantation operated from 1787 all the way up
until it burned down in 1835. The area was then purchased
by Mathias Day, Jr. in 1871 and a small community devel-

oped around the hotel he built there.

Local residents decided to name the new town after Day, and things really took off in the late 1880s when Henry Flagler's Florida East Coast Railroad started offering easy access to the area. Shortly after the turn of the century, Daytona Beach had already become a popular tourist destination that was earning the reputation as "The World's Most Famous Beach."

You also can't talk about the history of Daytona Beach without mentioning that the hard-packed sand here made it a popular spot for early auto races. There were a number of racing firsts that happened in Daytona Beach over the years, and any NASCAR fan will tell you how important "Daytona" is to their heart.

Attracting and entertaining tourists is the root of a major portion of the Daytona Beach lifestyle. The region plays host to two NASCAR races each year, as well as all kinds of auto-racing events. Then there are the huge Daytona Bike Week and Daytona Jeep Beach events that attract people from all over the globe.

But while many locals do participate in the fun during these busy weeks, it is important to realize that most year-round residents have a much calmer lifestyle that makes use of all of the local parks and beaches. You can do everything from standup paddle boarding in the Atlantic Ocean to hiking through the woods of Doris Leeper Spruce Creek Preserve.

Because it is one of the most popular destinations along Florida's Atlantic Coast, there is plenty of arts and culture to go around in Daytona, starting with historic landmarks like the Ponce Inlet Lighthouse.

Residents here can spend hours exploring destinations like the Halifax Historical Museum, the Museum of Arts & Sciences, and the Cici and Hyatt Brown Museum of Art. On top of that, there are always exciting performances happening at the Daytona Beach Bandshell, the Peabody Auditorium, and the Daytona Playhouse.

Many people think of Daytona Beach as just another tourist destination, but many who choose to retire here have realized that there is a whole lot more to Daytona than meets the eye.

Port Orange

Located just 15 minutes south of Daytona Beach, Port Orange is known for its small-town feel, but also for its close proximity to the big city amenities that residents can enjoy up in Daytona Beach, as well as in nearby Orlando.

The history of Port Orange dates back to 1804 when Spain granted 995 acres to Patrick Dean. Prior to that time, the area was home to Timucuan and Seminole Indians. Dean built a large plantation along the Halifax River, but his entire community was destroyed by the Seminole Indians.

Following the Civil War, a second attempt was made to settle the area by an abolitionist named John Milton Hawks, who was looking to create a home for 500 freed slaves. The area came to be known as Freedmanville but was officially named Orange Port by Hawks. In 1867, the name was changed to Port Orange, and the city as incorporated in 1926.

Like many of the small towns along the Atlantic Coast, the lifestyle you will find in Port Orange places a heavy emphasis on enjoying the outdoors, and particularly the beach.

Local parks like Spruce Creek Park offer great ways to enjoy the fabulous year-round climate, and there are also plenty of great options for fishing both from the shore and from local boat charters.

One of the most popular cultural attractions are the Dunlawton Sugar Mill Gardens, which is the last remaining portion of Patrick Dean's original plantation. History buffs will also enjoy a visit to Gamble Place Historic District.

Local concerts in Port Orange are typically held at the Kenneth Parker Amphitheater, but the community is also located just minutes from nearby Daytona Beach and only about an hour from Orlando, so there are plenty of additional cultural attractions nearby.

If you are in search of a great small-town community that is located right on the water, is close (but not too close) to big city amenities, Port Orange is one of the places you should be looking.

New Smyrna Beach

Just south of Port Orange is where you will find New Smyrna Beach. This beach town offers the atmosphere that many retirees are looking for, but also brings quite a few unique amenities to the table.

The first attempt to settle in the New Smyrna area happened all the way back in 1768, when Dr. Andrew Turnbull recruited 1,300 settlers to start his plantation community in Florida. Despite a promising start, the community was eventually destroyed by a combination of Indian attacks and disease.

After the last of Turnbull's settlers migrated north to St. Augustine, the area was sparsely populated all the way up until 1892 when Henry Flagler's Florida East Coast Railway established service to the community. Since then, New Smyrna Beach has been a popular destination for tourists, as well as the fishing and citrus industries.

Like most of the communities you will find along the Atlantic Coast, the lifestyle in New Smyrna Beach revolves around the great outdoors. Residents have a number of local parks available to them, including Flagler Avenue Park, Lake Ashby Park, Smyrna Dunes Park, and Doris Leeper Spruce Creek Preserve.

In addition to the local parks, residents also pass the time by taking advantage of the many fishing charters available, three different golf courses, tennis facilities, and taking in a race at the New Smyrna Speedway.

Many people would describe New Smyrna as a surf town, as it has some of the best waves the East Coast of Florida has to offer. But before you try to hang ten, be warned: New Smyrna is frequently cited as the "Shark Attack Capital of the World", as there are more shark bite incidents per square mile than on any other beach in the world.

Residents of New Smyrna Beach are known to have a tremendous amount of respect for local artists, which is why the community is known as one of "America's Top Small Cities for the Arts."

Between Gallerie di Vetro, the Atlantic Center for the Arts, and Arts on Douglas, there are multiple options to find local artists working on perfecting their craft.

New Smyrna Beach also has the advantage of being located less than 20 minutes south of Daytona Beach and about an hour from Orlando, so residents also have access to big city-style cultural experiences that are only a short drive from home.

The heart of the shopping scene in New Smyrna Beach is located along Flagler Avenue and Canal Street. Here you will find a collection of small shoppes and boutique stores that specialize in local, handmade items. For everyday shopping needs, there are a few strip malls located throughout the city.

With all kinds of great outdoor activities, plenty of culture and shopping, and some of the best restaurants you will find along the Atlantic Coast, New Smyrna Beach is one of the few places that meets and exceeds the expectations of just about everyone who visits.

Melbourne

Located in Brevard County, Melbourne is right in the middle of the Space Coast, just south of Cape Canaveral and about halfway between Daytona Beach and West Palm Beach.

Residents here enjoy close access to the Melbourne Orlando International Airport if that serves their needs, but they are also only a little over an hour away from the Orlando International Airport.

Of course, that means that all the other attractions and amenities of the greater Orlando area are only about an hour away.

Paleo-Indian artifacts and remains found in the area go way back in time, but the modern history of Melbourne started when the area was settled in 1877. The town was initially called Crane Creek, but was later renamed to honor its first postmaster, who came from Melbourne, Australia.

The most significant event in the early history of Melbourne was a massive fire that destroyed the original downtown district in 1919.

In 1942, the city grew tremendously after a large portion of land was used to establish Naval Air Station Melbourne, which because a major training facility for newly recruited pilots in both the Navy and Air Force during World War II. This land would later be converted into the Melbourne Orlando International Airport, which still operates today.

The local climate offers a hot and wet season from May through October, where the average high typically ranges from 96 to 102 degrees Fahrenheit. November to April is considered the warm and dry season, and those months see average highs from 89 to 97 degrees Fahrenheit.

Daily low temperatures can drop into the teens during the winter months in Melbourne, but the warmer months will feature comfortable evenings in the low 60s.

The most popular attraction for any town along the Space Coast will always be the Kennedy Space Center in Cape Canaveral. You will find it difficult to get tired of visiting this legendary destination.

Other popular activities in Melbourne include outdoor attractions like renting fishing charters, taking out standup paddle boards, and exploring many local parks and historic sites.

CENTRAL EAST COAST COMMUNITIES

Note: On my website I've got a handy list of all the communities mentioned in this book at: floridaforboomers.com/list

Huntington at Hunter's Ridge – Ormond Beach, FL

Located in the popular community of Ormond Beach, just north of Daytona Beach, Huntington at Hunter's Ridge is a maintenance-free community of 326 attached villas and single-family homes. The resort-style amenities that residents can enjoy here include a 12,500 square foot clubhouse with a fitness center and a beautiful outdoor pool that is surrounded by walking trails.

With multiple building companies to choose from, there are more than a dozen different floorplans to choose from at Huntington at Hunter's Ridge. Those homes can range in size from 1,517 square feet up to 2,235 square feet. Prices start around $300k.

55plusnewhomes.com

Ormond Renaissance – Ormond Beach, FL

Ormond Renaissance is expected to be a gated community of 280 condos across ten different buildings that is located in Ormond Beach. Amenities here include a 3,600 square foot clubhouse, state-of-the-art fitness center, resort-style pool, and plenty of community green spaces.

The condos at Ormond Renaissance are available in sizes ranging from 1,248 to 1,515 square feet. In last year's edition I wrote that Building 1 was sold out and pricing for Building 2 had not been released yet. Strangely that is still the current status at the time I'm updating this year. Most units in Building 1 sold in the $200k's or $300k's.

ormondrenaissance.com

Latitude Margaritaville – Daytona Beach, FL

Latitude Margaritaville is a Jimmy Buffet-themed community of more than 3,500 attached villas and single-family homes located in Daytona Beach that is a perfect destination for any "Parrothead".

Residents here enjoy access to amenities like the Fins Up! Fitness Center, a fantastic resort-style pool, and all the "boat drinks" they can handle from the Latitude Bar & Chill Restaurant. There's also a private beach club with shuttle service from the community.

Homes are available in many different sizes and styles ranging in size from about 1,200 sq. ft. to more than 2,500 sq. ft. Prices start in the $300k's.

latitudemargaritaville.com/daytona-beach

Venetian Bay - New Smyrna Beach, FL

Situated in one of Central Florida's favorite beach towns, New Smyrna Beach, Venetian Bay offers World Class Resort-Style amenities to its residents. Play a round of golf on the 18-Hole Championship golf course, spend a day with your family at the Beach and Swim Club, enjoy a relaxing day at the World Class Spa, stay active by joining the on-site fitness center or walking and biking on the miles of beautiful trails.

Residents also enjoy dining at the onsite restaurants. Venetian Bay features luxury estates in gated private communities; semi-custom homes; mid-sized single-family homes and duplexes; maintenance free luxury townhomes and apartment homes. Prices start in the $300k's.

venetianbay.info

Bridgewater at Viera – Melbourne, FL

Located in Melbourne, Bridgewater at Viera is a gated community of 875 attached and single-family homes. Amenities here will eventually include a 23,000 square foot clubhouse complex, a resort-style outdoor pool, and tennis courts.

Between the attached villas and the single-family homes, Bridgewater at Viera offers a total of five different floorplans to choose from that range in size from as little as 1,593 square feet all the way up to 2,807 square feet. Prices start in the $300k's.

lennar.com/new-homes/florida/treasure-coast-space-coast/melbourne/bridgewater-at-viera

Del Webb at Viera - Melbourne, FL

Situated over 500 acres, with plans for approximately 1,300 homes, Del Webb at Viera will offer retirement living in an acclaimed master-planned community known for its robust amenities and proximity to beautiful beaches, fine dining and shopping.

Del Webb at Viera will have single-family homes similar to those available in other Del Webb communities. At the time of this writing, pricing has yet to be released.

delwebb.com/homes/florida/orlando/melbourne/del-webb-at-viera-210834

Harmony Reserve – Vero Beach, FL

Harmony Reserve is a gated community of 397 attached and single-family homes that is located just outside of Vero Beach along Florida's popular Treasure Coast. Amenities here include everything from a 15,000 square foot clubhouse with a state-of-the-art fitness center to a huge outdoor pool surrounded by a collection of lakes and ponds.

Residents at Harmony Reserve can choose from six different attached villa floorplans and more than a dozen different single-family options. When you combine all of those models, this community can offer anywhere from 1,219 to 2,756 square feet. Pricing starts in the $400k's.

harmonyreserve.com

Aerial View of Boca Raton

PERHAPS BEST KNOWN for Miami and South Beach, Southeast Florida offers so much more. It has long been a retirement haven for people from the Northeast. Home prices in this region can be high, depending on the area. Major cities include Miami, Ft. Lauderdale, Hollywood, West Palm

Beach, Boca Raton, Delray Beach, and Stuart. Most people consider the Florida Keys to be a part of Southeast Florida as well.

Boca Raton

Considered by many to be the ultimate retirement destination, Boca Raton is located along the southeast coast of Florida just about equal distance between West Palm Beach to the north and Miami to the south.

This fantastic south Florida community boasts a tropical climate, easy access to international airports, and a nearly endless supply of golf courses...amongst other popular retirement activities. And that's not even starting on the classic Mediterranean architecture and the fabulous art museums!

The city of Boca Raton was originally settled in 1895, but things really started to take off during the Florida land boom in the 1920s. It was during that time that the first version of the famous Boca Raton Resort & Club was built, making Boca Raton a true resort destination.

By opening a manufacturing plant in the area during the 1960s, IBM was a key player in the development of the Boca Raton area. Since then, the city has grown into one of the most popular tourist destinations and retirement communities in all of Florida.

For many residents, the Boca Raton lifestyle revolves around country club activities like golf and tennis. With more than 30 different golf courses to choose from, you will never get tired of hitting the links.

Exploring the outdoors is another popular activity in Boca Raton. Residents are able to visit amazing beachfront parks like Red Reef Park, Spanish River Park, and South Inlet Park Beach. There are also other outdoor destinations to explore like Sugar Sand Park, Daggerwing Nature Center, and the amazing Gumbo Limbo Nature Center.

Boynton Beach

Located just about halfway between West Palm Beach and Boca Raton, Boynton Beach offers residents a lifestyle that is far-removed from all of the popular Florida tourist destinations without actually being all that far away from those places.

If you are the type of person who is looking to spend your retirement years enjoying the natural beauty of Florida by relaxing at the beach and chartering boats with your family in a relaxed environment, you are going to love what Boynton Beach has to offer!

The history of Boynton Beach dates all the way back to 1894 when Nathan Boynton came down from Port Huron Michigan and was so impressed by the tropical climate of the area that he decided to build a hotel. Despite the fact that Boynton died in 1911, the hotel bearing his name continued to operate in the town of Boynton for another 14 years all the way up until 1925.

In 1931, a community that broke away from the town of Boynton took on the name of Boynton Beach. However, when that community renamed itself "Ocean Ridge" in 1939, the town of Boynton elected to rename itself "Boynton Beach" just a few years later.

Boynton Beach Oceanfront Park is located just north of the original site of the Boynton Hotel and is one of the most attractive beaches you will find along Florida's Atlantic Coast. Spending even a short amount of time here strolling the boardwalk will quickly show why this park was named the best family beach in Palm Beach County.

Where Boynton Beach Oceanfront Park is known for calm and relaxing family fun, Boynton Harbor Marina is the place to go to have some fun! This is where you want to be if you are looking for fishing charters, scuba diving, sightseeing cruises, and jet ski rentals. If you can do it in a boat, you can do it here!

Just as the Oceanfront Park is family-focused in Boynton Beach, so is just about every aspect of the arts and culture scene that you will find throughout the community. The community is constant planning and hosting a wide range of art festival events, and there is also some truly stunning community art that you will find on display throughout the town.

With more than 81 current public art projects filling the streets of Boynton Beach, there is no shortage of love for the arts here!

If casual and relaxed are the two words that you want to define your retirement years, you will quickly find that Boynton Beach is just your speed.

Delray Beach

Located just an hour up the coast from Miami you will find Delray Beach, one of the best small-town communities in the entire country.

This is obvious to anyone who visits based solely on the number of art galleries, restaurants, and nightly entertainment events available throughout the popular downtown area. Delray Beach is the place where you can find big city culture in a small-town environment...which is why so many people have decided to make their homes here.

The town itself is comprised of 15.9 square miles in Palm Beach County, just a bit north of Boca Raton and bordered on the west by the Everglades. It is easily accessible by either by I-95 or Atlantic Avenue.

If being close to an airport is important to you, there are two to pick from near Delray Beach. The Palm Beach International Airport is just 15 miles north of town right off of I-95, and the Fort Lauderdale-Hollywood International Airport is located 30 miles south of Delray.

The Delray Beach area was originally settled in the 1800's and developed as a farm community. It officially became a town in 1911 and pineapple and tomato canning facilities were built shortly after that.

Like many Florida towns, it felt the boom of tourism and real estate speculation during the 1920s. During that time, many popular artists and writers decided to make their homes in

Delray Beach. This laid the groundwork for the thriving artist community that exists here today.

The final component that made Delray Beach as popular as it is today was the completion of Interstate 95 in the 1970's. Suddenly, this thriving community of arts and culture was accessible to anyone who wanted to visit.

Because arts and culture are such an important part of the community, Delray Beach is known for hosting many different annual festivals. Some of the most popular each year include Delray Affair, Garlic Fest, and the Delray Beach Wine & Seafood Festival. The town is also famous for the 100-foot Christmas tree it puts on display each year.

With this much art and culture packed into its 15 square miles, Delray Beach is the ultimate in sophisticated relaxation and the perfect place for any artist or aspiring artist to retire.

Delray might not get as much national attention as some of its neighbors but take a closer look and I think you'll see it deserves to be on your retirement radar.

Port St. Lucie

Port St. Lucie and other neighboring towns in St. Lucie County promote themselves as offering "the real Florida," which they describe as a perfect atmosphere for golf lovers or anyone looking for a small, friendly, beach town.

Located a little more than halfway from Daytona Beach to Miami, the town of Port St. Lucie offers a more relaxed feel than its much larger coastal counterparts, but it does so without asking residents to concede many of the same amenities!

Port St. Lucie is located on what is known as Florida's Treasure Coast, which got its name from a Spanish galleon fleet carrying treasure that was lost in a hurricane in 1715. With average January highs in the mid-70's and average August highs in the low 90's, this is the perfect location for anyone seeking a tropical climate, particularly during the winter months!

The area is also home to four different colleges that all share one campus, so education is widely available. If you need access to an airport, both the Treasure Coast Airpark and Naked Lady Ranch Airport are located less than 10 miles from Port St. Lucie.

In addition to Port St. Lucie, many visitors also like to explore nearby Fort Pierce and Hutchinson Island. Fort Pierce is known for having the feel of an "Old Florida" fishing village, and Hutchinson Island is a beach lover's paradise.

Port St. Lucie might just be the ideal location for people who love the game of golf. Here you will find the PGA Learning Center, the PGA Historical Center, the PGA Golf Professional Hall of Fame, and the Probst Library, which contains an unbelievable collection of golf archives.

Of course, Port St. Lucie isn't just a place for golf historians, there are also more than 20 different courses here that represent a wide range of quality and affordability. There are plenty of reasonably priced public courses for regular play, and there are also some PGA-level private courses as well!

Another reason that Port St. Lucie is such a popular location is that the New York Mets call it home from February to March every year for their spring training. Coming out to see the big-league squad during spring training can be an awesome experience, but residents also have the option to watch the Mets' high class-A minor league affiliate play here in Port St. Lucie throughout the summer!

While golf and baseball tend to take precedence in the Port St. Lucie area, there is no shortage of culture and history here either! The area contains attractions like the Port St. Lucie Botanical Gardens, a museum dedicated to the history of the US Navy SEALs, the Hallstrom Planetarium, the A.E. Backus Gallery and Museum, and the St. Lucie County Historical Museum. There are also a plethora of cultural events hosted as the Port St. Lucie Civic Center every year.

Port St. Lucie bills itself as perfect for golfers and anyone looking for a small, friendly beach town. If you fit into any of those categories, you will certainly enjoy spending your retirement here.

Stuart

Known as "The Sailfish Capital of the World," Stuart is located along the Atlantic Coast of Florida, north of West Palm Beach and just south of Port St. Lucie. This area of Florida is also known as "The Treasure Coast" because so many ships have been lost here fighting to survive storms over the years.

The area that would eventually become Stuart was once noted as "Gilbert's Bar" on nautical charts after the famous pirate, Pedro Gilbert. Legend has it that Gilbert would use the large sandbar outside of Stuart to hide his ship before chasing down and looting merchant ships.

In 1893, the area was named Potsdam by local landowner Otto Sypmann, who was originally from Potsdam, Germany. It was then renamed after Homer Hine Stuart, Jr. in 1895, following the completion of the Florida East Coast Railway.

You aren't likely to find any Pirates strolling through Stuart these days, but the lifestyle here still starts and ends with the beach and the water. On any given day, you are almost certain to find residents enjoying themselves at Stuart Beach, Sandsprit Park, and Bathtub Reef.

If you are looking to explore some inland waterways or take in some local wildlife, Halpatiokee Regional Park is definitely the place you are going to want to start. And don't forget about all of the local fishing charter companies that will gladly show you why Stuart is known as "The Sailfish Capital of the World!"

The Florida Keys

The Florida Keys is perfect whether visiting for a weekend or deciding to make it a permanent home.

An idyllic tropical setting at the tip of the United States combined with a myriad of recreation, entertainment, and cultural opportunities create the ideal place to spend the next stage in life.

You can certainly get to the Keys by boat. In fact, before the 1910's and the completion of Henry Flagler's Overseas Railway, boats were the only way to get to the Keys.

U.S. 1 is the only road in and out of the Keys. The Keys begin about 15 miles south of Miami. From that point it's about 3.5 hours to drive all the way to the bottom of the Keys in Key West. You can also get to the Keys by plane. Both commercial and private planes use either Key West International Airport, or the Florida Keys Marathon International Airport.

Downtown Key West

The steady climate of the Florida Keys is a secret known to residents. The temperatures in the winter rarely get below the 60s. Summer heat is not a problem because the ocean helps to keep the temperatures of many cities in the Keys in the 80s.

Most people are surprised to hear this, as it does not sound like the weather in other parts of Florida at all. Where I live, in Central Florida, we regularly get up into the mid to high 90's in the summer, and there are times when we experience the teens and twenties during the winter. Granted, some people like to experience the different seasons, but if you prefer steady ideal weather all year 'round, the Keys might be for you.

Into every life some rain must fall, but the rain usually waits until the summer to fall in the Keys. When the rain does fall, it usually takes the form of short-lived thunderstorms in the afternoons. Few days are complete rainouts. The winter months are the driest months, only experiencing brief rains, if any.

Some people are concerned about hurricanes when considering a move to the Florida Keys. Hurricanes do not hit the Keys every year, and when they do, it will likely be in the late summer months.

Preparation is the key to avoiding serious damage to property, and with hurricanes, time to prepare is given. Weather forecasters usually provide ample time before a storm hits to prepare a home and evacuate, if needed. This means that Keys residents are never caught off guard. The local building codes are such so that most newer homes will ride out many of the tropical systems that pass through the Keys. We'll talk more about hurricanes later in the book.

One downside during hurricane season though is that whenever a big hurricane threatens the Keys, residents and visitors are urged to evacuate. Sounds simple enough, but it can get a little hectic with one road in, and one road out of the Keys (U.S. 1).

Though it rests at the tip of Florida, the Keys maintains its own identity when it comes to the arts. Museums abound in the Keys, focusing on such diverse topics as the history of diving, Ernest Hemingway and shipwrecks.

Several live theater groups make the Florida Keys their home. The Keys Players, the Waterfront Playhouse, the Red Barn Theatre, and the Tennessee Williams Theatre are just a few of the options for catching a live performance. These groups provide a wide range of genres in their performances, ensuring that there will be something to suit the tastes of every theatergoer.

The Florida Keys are full of history. Historic sites around the Keys convey this to visitors. Many residents neglect to spot these gems in the rough, but for anyone newly transplanted to the Keys a trip to the historic sites will give a full picture of the area.

Harry Truman's "Little White House" in Key West is Florida's only presidential museum. Fans of Ernest Hemingway will want to make a stop at his home which is also in Key West. Other museums focusing on the history and culture of the Florida Keys should be regular destinations for any resident with an interest in history.

The Florida Keys have nearly limitless recreation options. Beaches abound in the Keys where fishing, swimming, snorkeling, and diving can be enjoyed. Nature preserves and parks provide a quiet getaway for hiking or birdwatching. Indian Key state park, Fort Zachary Taylor state park, San Pedro underwater archaeological preserve state park, the Lignumvitae Key Botanical State Park, and the Crane Point nature center are available for recreation for residents and visitors alike.

While most people visit this website in search of Florida retirement communities, you won't find many (if any?) dedicated retirement communities in the Florida Keys like you see in other parts of the state. But there are some great communities, nonetheless.

Moving to the Florida Keys requires prior planning and thought put into the decision, but once people move to the Keys, they often wonder why they did not do it sooner.

SOUTHEAST FLORIDA COMMUNITIES

Note: On my website I've got a handy list of all the communities mentioned in this book at:
floridaforboomers.com/list

Avalon Trails – Delray Beach, FL

Avalon Trails is a 55+ active adult community located in Delray Beach, FL.

At the heart of the community is The Club at Avalon Trails, which will feature a resort-style pool and adjacent lap pool, a fully equipped fitness studio, card rooms, a cafe, community garden, walking trails, tennis courts, pickleball courts, and more.

The homes at Avalon Trails will include 2 and 3 bedroom villas and single family homes that include features like granite countertops, stainless steel appliances, and hurricane impact windows and doors. Prices start in the $400k's.

lennar.com/new-homes/florida/palm-beach/delray-beach/avalon-trails

Cresswind Palm Beach at Westlake – Westlake, FL

Cresswind Palm Beach at Westlake is an active adult community located in Westlake, FL between Wellington and Palm Beach Gardens. The clubhouse offers residents a place to gather and participate in social activities facilitated by a full-time Lifestyle Director.

Outdoor amenities include pickleball & tennis courts, walking trails, resort-style pool and spa, resistance pool, dog park, event and entertainment areas. Prices start in the $400k's.

kolterhomes.com/new-homes/westlake-florida-active-adult-cresswind-palm-beach/

Cresswind at PGA Village Verano – Port St. Lucie, FL

Cresswind at PGA Village Verano is a community of villas and single-family homes in Port St. Lucie. The amenities here include access to the 27,000 square foot clubhouse, indoor and outdoor pools, a state-of-the-art fitness center, a dog park, and an enormous pickleball complex.

Cresswind at PGA Village Verano offers 18 different villa and single-family home options, and prices start in the $300k's.

kolterhomes.com/new-homes/port-saint-lucie-florida-active-adult-pga-village-verano/

Del Webb Tradition – Port St. Lucie, FL

Located in beautiful Port St. Lucie, Del Web Tradition is a gated community of 550 attached and single-family homes that began construction in 2017. Amenities here include a large clubhouse, resort-style outdoor pool, and a state-of-the-art fitness center.

The attached homes at Del Webb Tradition clock in at 1,579 square feet and are available with either two or three bedrooms. The single-family homes range in size from 1,671 to 2,589 square feet and are available with two to four bedrooms. Prices start in the $300k's.

delwebb.com/homes/florida/treasure-coast/port-st-lucie/del-webb-tradition-209846

Esplanade at Tradition - Port St. Lucie, FL

Esplanade at Tradition is a new 55+ resort-style community in Port St. Lucie, in the 8,300-acre Tradition master-planned community.

Single family homes here range in size from about 1,600 to 2,900 sq. ft. And prices start in the high $300k's.

taylormorrison.com/fl/treasure-coast/port-st-lucie/esplanade-at-tradition

Falls at Parkland - Parkland, FL

This 55+ active lifestyle community features a resort-style pool, lounge area, and many recreational activities, including pickleball. There's also a state-of-the-art fitness center and yoga room.

There are 6 single-family home floorplans available ranging in size from about 1,700 to 2,600 sq. ft. Prices start in the $600k's.

ryanhomes.com/new-homes/communi-ties/10222120151585/florida/parkland/falls-at-parkland

Four Seasons at Parkland – Parkland, FL

Located just a bit north of Fort Lauderdale, Four Seasons at Parkland is a luxury community of 538 single-family homes built around 12 beautiful lakes. Amenities here include a 25,000 square foot clubhouse, state-of-the-art fitness center, two resort-style pools, and a tennis pro shop.

Four Seasons at Parkland offers 14 different floorplans that range in size from 1,965 square feet all the way up to 3,615 square feet. Prices start in the $800k's.

khov.com/find-new-homes/florida/parkland/33076/four-seasons/k-hovnanians-four-seasons-at-parkland-50s

The Grand at Veranda Preserve – Port St. Lucie, FL

The Grand at Veranda Preserve is a new, resort-style community in Port St. Lucie designed for residents "55 & Better" from Lennar Homes. Amenities include a private Clubhouse with social spaces, resort-style pool with lap area and wet decks, poolside bar, state of the-art fitness center, tennis, pickleball, and bocce ball courts, event lawn, and more.

There are three classes of models at Verandah Preserve, ranging in size from 1,410 sq. ft. of living space to just over 2,800 sq. ft. of living space. Prices start in the $500k's.

lennar.com/new-homes/florida/treasure-coast-space-coast/port-st-lucie/veranda-preserve/the-grand

Regency at Avenir – Palm Beach Gardens, FL

Regency at Avenir is a 55+, active-adult community in Palm Beach Gardens offering resort-style amenities and a low-maintenance lifestyle.

Regency at Avenir's private amenities will include a resort-style swimming pool and spa, state-of-the-art fitness and wellness center, a yoga studio, tennis, pickleball and bocce courts, a golf simulator, an art room with kiln, a ballroom, cafe, outdoor amphitheater, and more.

469 single-family homes are planned for Regency at Avenir, ranging in size from 1,800 to 2,800 square feet. Prices start in the $600k's.

tollbrothers.com/luxury-homes-for-sale/Florida/Regency-at-Avenir

Valencia Grand – Boynton Beach, FL

Valencia Grand in Boynton Beach offers truly premium 55+ living unlike anywhere else, with a prime South Florida location, sophisticated country-club lifestyle, and all-new unmatched amenities. Valencia Grand takes sophisticated living to the next level with one-story home designs made for 55+ living with stand-out features including expansive high ceilings, transom windows that let in even more Florida sunshine, impressive gourmet kitchens, spa-like baths, spacious outdoor living areas and more starting from the $900k's.

glhomes.com/valencia-grand/

Valencia Walk at Riverland – Port St. Lucie, FL

Valencia Walk at Riverland is one of the newest 55+ communities on Florida's East Coast. Located in Port St. Lucie, Valencia Walk at Riverland is the third 55+ community from GL Homes in the Riverland master plan community.

At this new community, residents can walk to nearby shops and restaurants, spend the day at the beach or simply enjoy all the amenities right within your own neighborhood. Prices start in the $400k's.

glhomes.com/valencia-walk-at-riverland/

Veranda Preserve - Port St. Lucie, FL

Veranda Preserve is a new, resort-style community in Port St. Lucie designed for residents "55 & Better" from Lennar Homes. Amenities include a private Clubhouse with social spaces, resort-style pool with lap area and wet decks, poolside bar, state-of-the-art fitness center, tennis, pickleball, and bocce ball courts, event lawn, and more.

There are three classes of models at Verandah Preserve, ranging in size from 1,410 sq. ft. of living space to just over 2,800 sq. ft. of living space. Prices start in the $300k's.

lennar.com/new-homes/florida/treasure-coast/port-st-lucie/veranda-preserve

EDITOR'S NOTE: All of the content for this chapter was written before Hurricane Ian passed through Southwest Florida in September 2022. I'm pleased to report though that just two months later in November 2022, most areas affected are bouncing back quickly.

This region is popular with people from the Midwest U.S. who can hop on I-75 and shoot right down to Florida. Popular destinations in Southwest Florida include Naples, Marco Island, Cape Coral, Port Charlotte, and Fort Myers. Home prices in some of these cities are known to be among the highest in the state, but the beauty of the area may be unrivaled.

Bonita Springs

Located about halfway between Fort Myers and Naples, Bonita Springs is a beachfront community along the southern

Gulf Coast of Florida that is perfect for dog lovers, fishing enthusiasts, and anyone looking to embrace outdoor activities.

Because it fits somewhere in between small-town community and booming tourist destination, Bonita Springs offers a unique hybrid of calm serenity and exciting amenities that ends up making it a perfect fit for many retirees.

People began visiting Bonita Springs via the Fort Myers-Southern Railroad in the 1920s, but the big boom really happened following the opening of Interstate 75. After that, the town grew right along with its population as it quickly evolved into the Bonita Springs you will find there today.

Heading to the beach is what life in Bonita Springs is all about, and one of the most popular places to do just that is the Bonita Springs Public Beach. Here you will find miles and miles of beautiful white sand beaches that are perfectly made for doing absolutely nothing.

If you happen to be a dog lover, you can plan on being a regular visitor to Dog Beach, which is one of just a few leash-free, dog-friendly beaches in the state. Your four-legged friends will have a blast here running through the sand and swimming in the Gulf!

The arts and culture scene in Bonita Springs doesn't compare to what you might find nearby in Fort Myers or Naples, but the beauty of living here is that you are always just a short drive away from those booming cultural centers.

One cultural attraction that many residents appreciate is the Centers for the Arts Bonita Springs. Here you will find the combination of the Center for Visual Arts and the Center for Performing Arts, which covers most of the bases for anyone looking to network with other art lovers.

With just the right amount of amenities mixed into one of the most relaxing environments along the Gulf Coast, Bonita Springs is the perfect destination for anyone looking to enjoy their retirement years in peace and quiet.

Fort Myers

Known for offering the perfect combination of recreation and relaxation, Fort Myers contains an endless amount of options including white sand beaches, first-class golf courses, exciting deep-sea fishing, and outstanding shopping.

There is an amazing selection of great local restaurants in just about every neighborhood, and baseball fans will be excited to know that both the Boston Red Sox and the Minnesota Twins host their spring training activities here.

Fort Myers is the hub of activity in Southwest Florida and is located only 10 miles from the Southwest Florida International Airport. If you are looking for the perfect community along the southern Gulf Coast of Florida, Fort Myers is the place where you want to start your search!

The community is actually located a bit inland from the Gulf along the Caloosahatchee River. The closest interstate highway is I-75, which runs just east of the city and can take you south towards Naples or north towards Port Charlotte and then up to Sarasota.

Just west of Fort Myers is where you will find the popular destinations of Pine Island, Cayo Costa, Captiva, and of course, Sanibel Island.

Fort Myers was originally settled in 1866 when Manuel A. Gonzalez brought his family here from Key West. It became home to one of the first forts along the Caloosahatchee River and was an important location during the Seminole Wars.

In the late 1800s and early 1900s, the area gained popularity when both Thomas Edison and Henry Ford built winter homes in Fort Myers. Quite a few local landmarks still bear the names of these two American legends.

Like most of southwest Florida, Fort Myers is known for having a great year-round climate. The average temperature throughout the year is 84 degrees Fahrenheit. Those temperatures generally reach up into the 90s during the summer months and it is common to see highs in the mid-70s during the winter months.

Naples

Like many southwest Florida communities, Naples brings together the best of shopping, recreation, and beautiful white sand beaches. But residents here would definitely argue that Naples offers the best versions of all three.

Historic downtown Naples is filled with high-end shoppes and boutiques. The surrounding areas are littered with championship level golf courses. And this location along the southern Gulf Coast of Florida boasts some of the most stunning beaches you will find anywhere.

Naples is located just under an hour straight south of Fort Myers, and about half an hour north of Marco Island. This makes Naples the southernmost metropolitan area along the Gulf Coast of Florida.

There is a small municipal airport located right in Naples, but the closest major airport is located about 30 miles north in Fort Myers. As for local highways, US-41 runs right through the heart of town and I-75 is the closest Interstate.

With Fort Myers and Everglades National Park both so close to Naples, residents have the option of heading north to access the rest of Florida or east to venture into the relaxing wilderness of the Everglades.

Naples was founded by a US Senator named John Stuart Williams and a newspaper owner from Louisville named Walter Halderman in the 1880's. Many people referred to the area as Naples because of its similarities to the city of Naples in Italy, which is known for its waterfront location and mild climate. The name stuck and after World War II the city really began to grow quickly.

Being the southernmost Gulf Coast retirement destination, Naples residents enjoy a moderate climate that is a few degrees warmer than its northern counterparts for most of the year.

Residents can expect to see average daily highs in the low 90's during the summer months and in the high 70's during the winter months. Even in the winter months, the average low never falls below the low 50's.

Cape Coral

Just across the way from Fort Myers is the quiet community of Cape Coral, which offers up the ideal destination for many retirees.

With more than 400 miles of canals and an equally impressive number of outstanding golf courses, Cape Coral is a prime destination for anything water-related, and the golfing is top-notch as well.

The history of Cape Coral is relatively short compared to some of the other cities across the state of Florida. The area was purchased by Leonard and Jack Rosen after they flew over it in 1957. With the blessing of Lee County officials, the brothers set out to build one of the state's early master-planned communities, which they called Redfish Point.

As the area grew in popularity throughout the 1960s, people began referring to Redfish Point as "the Cape," which eventually evolved into "Cape Coral." That growth has continued for years, and it is actually increasing today after the city was recently named one of the "Best Places to Retire" by Forbes Magazine.

Because it isn't as famous as some of the neighboring cities, Cape Coral has been able to maintain a very relaxed lifestyle despite its tremendous track record of growth. And because it is a master-planned community, you will find a great selection of parks that all seem to be located in just the right places.

One of the original landmarks of the city is Yacht Club Community Park, which is located right on the Caloosahatchee River. This is a great spot to put a boat into the water, but even non-boaters will enjoy fishing from the pier or taking a dip in the community pool.

For golfers, Coral Oaks Golf Course is the place to relax. This Arthur Hills designed course features 8 lakes and 37 bunkers, which combine to make it both challenging and beautiful.

While Cape Coral doesn't have a long history, it does have a history that has been well-documented thanks to the Cape Coral Historical Museum. In addition to documenting the local history, the museum also boasts an impressive rose garden that is a must-see for all flower-lovers.

The area is also home to the Southwest Florida Military Museum & Library, as well as the Cape Coral Arts Studio. When you combine these local destinations with the thriving theater scene located in nearby Fort Myers, there is plenty of history and culture to go around in Cape Coral.

When you combine a wide range of great dining options with plenty of parks and golf courses and a bit of culture, you end up with the relaxing combination of Cape Coral. And that is what makes this destination the perfect option for retirees looking for a calmer alternative to Fort Myers.

Port Charlotte

Located almost exactly halfway between Sarasota and Fort Myers, Port Charlotte is one of the true hidden gems of Florida's Gulf Coast, which makes it a natural destination for those looking to enjoy their retirement years.

This small town is located right on the water of Charlotte Harbor and offers access to more than 165 miles of waterway, so all kinds of water activities are extremely popular here.

When the Florida Land Boom took off following World War II, it was only natural that Port Charlotte would appeal to enterprising developers, and the area quickly became the most popular town in Charlotte County. That population growth continued to expand throughout the 70s, 80s, and 90s.

With a whopping 830 miles of shoreline, everything about the Port Charlotte lifestyle revolves around the water. The area regularly ranks as one of the world's best sailing destinations, and there are more than two dozen local marinas that make storing and maintaining boats of all sizes easy.

In addition to taking a sailboat out on the open seas, local residents also enjoy other water activities like canning, kayaking, and standup paddleboarding. There are more than 200 miles of mangrove tunnel waterways that work their way through Charlotte County, so residents never run out of places to explore.

Port Charlotte residents also have more than 20 outstanding golf courses to choose from across Charlotte County and some of the most secluded white sand beaches in all of Florida, so finding a tee time or a suntan spot is never an issue.

The cultural side of Port Charlotte revolves around the happenings of the Cultural Center of Charlotte County. Since it opened in 1960, this has been the local hub of activity for the artist community offering everything from clubs and classes to performances and expos.

One of the biggest draws to the Cultural Center of Port Charlotte are the regular performances put on by the Charlotte Players, which is one of the oldest performing arts organizations in all of Florida.

If small town living mixed with boats, golf courses, and beaches is what you are looking for, Port Charlotte might be the perfect destination. And when you add in the culture, shopping, and dining options, it all adds up to one of the best-kept secrets in all of Florida.

SOUTHWEST FLORIDA COMMUNITIES

Note: On my website I've got a handy list of all the communities mentioned in this book at:
floridaforboomers.com/list

Cascades at River Hall – Alva, FL

Cascades at River Hall occupies over 2,000 acres of beautiful land just outside of Fort Myers, Florida. The community plan here calls for around 575 single-family homes, as well as a host of amenities like a community clubhouse, outdoor pool, and fitness center. Residents here also have the option of joining the Davis Love III 18-hole golf course for an annual fee.

With multiple builders that each offer a selection of styles and floorplans, the options are nearly unlimited at Cascades at River Hall. Those choices can be as small as 1,500 square feet, or they can range up towards a more comfortable 2,800 square feet. Prices start in the $300k's.

drhorton.com/florida/southwest-florida/alva/cascades-at-river-hall

Del Webb Oak Creek - Fort Myers

Del Webb Oak Creek is a new 55+ community that just opened in Fort Myers in 2022. Here you'll find pretty much the same floorplans and amenities offered in other Del Webb communities. Prices start in the $300k's.

delwebb.com/homes/florida/fort-myers/north-fort-myers/del-webb-oak-creek-210706

Del Webb Naples – Ave Maria, FL

Del Webb Naples is a massive community of 2,000 attached and single-family homes located in the even larger master-planned community of Ave Maria. Residents here can enjoy amenities like the 12,000 square foot Oasis Club and the Panther Run Golf Club, plus they also have access to a number of additional amenities in the Ave Maria community.

Homes at Del Webb Naples range in size from 1,438 to 2,611 square feet depending on whether you are looking for a smaller attached villa or a larger single-family home. Prices start in the $300k's.

delwebb.com/homes/florida/naples/ave-maria/del-webb-naples-11885

Valencia Trails – Naples, FL

Valencia Trails in Naples, FL offers the best resort lifestyle with a magnificent 42,000 sq. ft. Clubhouse where every day new events, clubs, and entertainment abound. Relax by the pool, grab a bite at the restaurant, catch a show in the social hall, or take a relaxing stroll or jog along the community's iconic trails. The options are endless!

Designed for 55+ living, the gorgeous contemporary style single-family homes at Valencia Trails offer the ultimate in style, convenience, and luxury with spacious living areas, impressive gourmet kitchens, and screened and covered patios to make the most of Florida's beautiful weather year-round. Come home to luxurious standard features including tile roof, brick pavers, stainless steel and gas appliances, designer tile flooring throughout main areas, rich stone exterior finishes and so much more. Prices start in the $600k's.

glhomes.com/valencia-trails/

CHAPTER ELEVEN
CENTRAL WEST COAST

TAMPA, St. Petersburg, Clearwater, Bradenton, and Sarasota are the biggest populations centers in this region of the state. Also known as the Gold Coast, the west coast of Florida offers direct access to the Gulf of Mexico, which is perhaps a more serene option than the Atlantic Ocean.

Crystal River

Crystal River is located right on the Gulf Coast of Florida just a little over an hour north of Tampa, a little over an hour south of Gainesville, and about an hour and a half west of Orlando. This area is commonly referred to as "The Nature Coast" because of the abundance of parks, preserves, and wildlife, and it is also one of the best places to get up close and personal with some West Indian Manatees.

Crystal River is also known for all of the natural springs that produce warm water year-round. This is what attracts all of the manatees, and also what produces some of the best natural environments in all of Florida that are open for locals to explore freely.

Human life in Crystal River tracks back as far as 500 BC. At that time, the area was home to many Native Americans that were known for building large mounds of discarded shellfish shells. However, the area was abandoned prior to being discovered by European settlers.

During the era of the Civil War, the turpentine business was big in Crystal River. That was followed by the discovery and production of phosphate during the time of World War II. Today, the area is known for having some of the best tarpon fishing in the world and being a calm and relaxing place for nature lovers to retire.

The lifestyle in Crystal River revolves around enjoying all of the state parks, wildlife preserves, and open waters that local residents have access to. Whether you are looking to swim with the manatees, explore the area's history, or catch and cook your own seafood, there are plenty of options in Crystal River.

As you begin to explore the area, you will definitely want to check out Three Sisters Springs, the Crystal River National Wildlife Refuge, the Crystal River Archaeological State Park, and Fort Island Trail Park. Each of these local attractions offer a unique version of the nature-lover lifestyle that Crystal River is known for.

Crystal River offers residents almost endless opportunities for hiking, boating, fishing, birding, and many other types of nature experiences. The entire area revolves around the idea that getting close to nature is what life is all about.

Sarasota/Bradenton

These two are often spoken of in the same breath, and because they are so close in proximity we've lumped them together.

Located along the Gulf Coast just an hour south of Tampa and a little under two hours north of Fort Myers you will find the historic artist towns of Sarasota and Bradenton. Both of these communities combine the historic Old Florida feel with vibrant cultural districts to create one of the most perfect atmospheres anywhere.

While they are separate communities, both Sarasota and Bradenton feature rich historic roots, a great cultural community, and a wonderfully calm pace of life.

Sarasota was originally formed in 1902, but really took off when Charles Ringling (of Ringling Bros. Circus fame) began investing in the area in the 1920s. Despite dying soon after finishing construction on his waterfront mansion, Ringling had a lasting impact on the area.

The key figure in the history of Bradenton was Dr. Joseph Braden, who's house in the area was more like a fort that would protect local settlers from the Seminole Indians. There are multiple historic buildings still standing in Bradenton today that date back to the 1800s.

With both of these towns located so close together, they have virtually identical climates. Like most of Florida, this area is known for being hot in the summer and warm in the winter.

The average high in January is just over 70 degrees Fahrenheit, and the average high in the summer months is just over 90 degrees Fahrenheit.

Both Sarasota and Bradenton have thriving cultural communities, so things like art studios, theater performances, and boutique shopping are very popular here.

One of the biggest attractions in the Sarasota area is the Ringling Museum of Art. The community also hosts annual events like The Ringling International Arts Festival, The Sarasota Film Festival, The Sarasota Music Festival, and The Sarasota Blues Fest.

Up in Bradenton, the cultural community is centered around the Village of the Arts, which contains about 30 different artist galleries and studios. There is also plenty of exciting entertainment happening regularly at The Riverwalk along the Manatee River.

St. Petersburg

Aerial view of St Petersburg

Across the bay from Tampa and just south of Clearwater is where you will find the city of St. Petersburg. Known for offering the perfect combination of white sand beaches, crystal clear water, and all of the big city amenities that make life enjoyable, St. Petersburg is the perfect destination for anyone who wants a little bit of everything in their retirement lifestyle.

The city of St. Petersburg was founded by John C. Williams and Peter Demens back in the late 1800s. Williams purchased the land that would become the city in 1875, and Demens brought the first railroad to town in 1888.

According to local legend, the two founders flipped a coin to determine who would choose a name for the new city.

Demens won the coin toss and elected to name their city after his hometown in Russia. As a consolation prize, Williams was able to name the first hotel in town after his hometown of Detroit.

During the 1950s and 1960s, St. Petersburg saw a tremendous amount of growth after the construction of multiple bridges that made it much more accessible from the mainland.

With its role as one of the three major cities in the Tampa - St. Petersburg - Clearwater metropolitan area, the lifestyle in St. Pete offers the perfect combination of big city amenities and beautiful beaches. The local beaches here offer picture-perfect white sand and clear water and can be visited all year round.

Residents often start their beach going fun at St. Pete Beach, but they also have the option to explore nearby Clearwater Beach, as well as some of the local islands like Honeymoon Island and Caladesi Island. Then there are all of the great parks and preserves in the area like Sawgrass Lake Park, Vinoy Park, and Weedon Island Preserve.

With its big city amenities, there is no shortage of culture to be found in St. Pete. You can spend days and days exploring local museums and galleries like The Dali Museum, Duncan McClellan Gallery, and the Florida Holocaust Museum.

There is also an astounding number of theaters throughout the city. Between the Freefall Theatre, Mahaffey Theater, American Stage Theatre Company, and The Palladium at St.

Petersburg College, you can find a great performance almost any night of the week.

Those who choose to retire in St. Petersburg are people who want the best of both worlds. They enjoy the luxuries that come with city life, but they are also drawn to the peaceful beauty of a relaxing day at the beach. If you find yourself equally drawn to both, then this might be the perfect place for you.

Tampa

As the third largest city in the state of Florida, Tampa offers residents all of the big city amenities they are looking for combined with the fantastic climate that draws people to the Sunshine State in the first place. In addition to tons of amenities and great weather, Tampa is also located right on the water and filled with outstanding shopping and dining options.

The name Tampa comes from the Native American tribe that originally called this area home. Its literal translation is "sticks of fire." The name was a reference to the many lightning storms that occur here during the summer months.

Before the 1880s, the town of Tampa was just a small fishing outpost. However, the discovery of phosphate in the area combined with the arrival of railroad transportation turned Tampa into a boomtown overnight, and it was one of Florida's largest cities by 1900.

No matter what you are passionate about, you can find a way to pursue those passions all over this large city. Some of the best lifestyle benefits you will find here include experiences like visiting Busch Gardens Tampa, the Florida Aquarium, and Lowry Park Zoo.

In addition to those major attractions, residents also love kicking back and relaxing at places like Lettuce Lake Regional Park or Curtis Hixon Waterfront Park. And if that still isn't enough, you can follow the city's three professional sports teams all year round.

As with any major city, there is an endless number of cultural opportunities to explore throughout Tampa. The Henry B. Plant Museum is a fascinating experience that explains the significance of Plant's famous railroad coming to town. Then there are the amazing museum experiences at the Tampa Bay History Center, the Museum of Science and Industry, and the Tampa Museum of Art.

If your cultural desires are more theatrical, you will appreciate the beautiful Tampa Theatre and The Straz Performing Arts Center. Both provide amazing settings for your favorite plays, musicals, and operas.

Whether you prefer to live right in the heart of the city or out in the suburbs, there is no denying that the Tampa area is overflowing with opportunity and excitement. And that is exactly why the third largest city in Florida continues to grow at such a rapid pace!

Venice

Located just south of Sarasota, but not quite as far south as Fort Myers or Sanibel Island, Venice sits in a sweet spot along

Florida's southern Gulf Coast that makes it the perfect destination for anyone looking to make the most of 14 miles of stunning white sand beaches.

In addition to those beautiful beaches, Venice is also known for all kinds of exciting ways to enjoy the great outdoors. It is a fabulous destination for those interested in exploring arts and culture, boutique shopping, or a wide range of outstanding restaurant choices.

The area that would eventually become Venice, Florida was originally named Horse and Chaise. However, it was renamed by Frank Higel in 1888 because it reminded him of Venice, Italy where he spent time as a child.

Sometime around 1916, John Nolan was brought in as a city planner to turn this naturally beautiful area into a well-planned Gulf Coast paradise. Then, when the area was connected to nearby Tampa and Miami in the early 1920s, the population began to grow at a rapid pace.

Venice was also the winter home of the famous Ringling Brothers Barnum & Bailey Circus during the 1950s, and the creation of the Intracoastal Waterway in the 1960s attracted even more people to the area.

Everything about the Venice lifestyle revolves around enjoying the great outdoors in one way or another. There are so many different parks tucked into various corners of town that even the most experienced locals have trouble making use of all of them.

Residents have their choice of great options like taking their dogs to Paw Park, enjoying daily music at the gazebo or splashing in the fountain at Centennial Park, taking the children to enjoy Legacy Park, playing shuffleboard at Hecksher Park, or checking out The Venice Arboretum at West Blalock Park.

A favorite pastime of both locals and tourists is shark tooth hunting. Venice bills itself as "The Shark Tooth Capital of the World" and celebrates that designation with an annual Sharks' Tooth Festival. There is also a wealth of history and culture on display at the Venice Museum & Archives and The Venice Art Center.

With all kinds of outdoor activities, a first-class arts and culture scene, great boutique shopping, and more than a few excellent restaurants, it isn't hard to see why Venice is such a popular choice among retirees looking to relocate along the Gulf Coast.

CENTRAL WEST COAST COMMUNITIES

Note: On my website I've got a handy list of all the communities mentioned in this book at: floridaforboomers.com/list

Cascades at Southern Hills – Brooksville, FL

Cascades at Southern Hills is an age-restricted gated neighborhood of nearly 200 single-family homes inside the larger master-planned community of Southern Hills Plantation about an hour south of Tampa. Amenities here include a neighborhood clubhouse, as well as the opportunity to purchase access to all of the many amenities of Southern Hills Plantation.

New construction at Cascades at Southern Hills is currently available in seven different floorplans ranging from about 1,500 to 2,335 square feet. Prices were unavailable at the time of this writing.

inlandhomes.com/new-homes/tampa/cascades/

Cresswind at Lakewood Ranch – Lakewood Ranch, FL

Cresswind at Lakewood Ranch is a 250-acre community of 650 single-family homes located just east of Sarasota and Bradenton. Amenities here include a huge community clubhouse, resort-style swimming pool, and access to additional amenities in the larger Lakewood Ranch community.

New homes at Cresswind at Lakewood Ranch are all single-floorplan models that range in size from two to four bedrooms with an optional upstairs bonus room. Prices start in the $400k's.

kolterhomes.com/new-homes/sarasota-bradenton-cresswind-lakewood-ranch/

Cypress Falls at The Woodlands – North Port, FL

Cypress Falls at The Woodlands is a gated community of 710 attached and single-family homes in North Port, Florida, which is about halfway between Sarasota and Fort Myers. Residents here enjoy access to amenities like a community clubhouse, resort-style pool, and a putting green.

New construction is available here for either attached or single-family homes. The attached homes range in size from 1,362 to 1,651 square feet. Then the single-family options are a little bigger ranging from 1,372 to 1,968 square feet. Prices start in the $300k's.

delwebb.com/homes/florida/sarasota/north-port/cypress-falls-at-the-woodlands-209208

Del Webb Bay View - Parrish/Sarasota

Del Webb Bay View is located in Parrish, which is in Manatee County, about 30 minutes away from downtown Sarasota, St. Petersburg, and Tampa. Like most Del Webb communities, residents can expect resort-style amenities hosted by a full-time lifestyle director. Even though this community only just recently opened, I've already had a few readers purchase homes there.

Single family homes and villas are available in sizes ranging from 1,500 sq. ft. to more than 3,300 sq. ft. Prices start in the $300k's.

delwebb.com/homes/florida/sarasota/parrish/del-webb-bayview-210515

Del Webb Bexley – Land O' Lakes, FL

Del Webb Bexley is a fairly new gated community of 850 single-family homes just north of Tampa. Amenities here will include a 17,000 square foot clubhouse with a state-of-the-art fitness center, a resort-style outdoor pool, a full-time activities director, and a homeowners' associate to take care of general maintenance.

New homes at Del Webb Bexley are available in three different series that each offer three different floor plans. Altogether, those nine floor plans range in size from 1,372 square feet all the way up to 2,852 square feet. Prices start in the high $300k's.

delwebb.com/homes/florida/tampa/land-o-lakes/del-webb-bexley-209960

Del Webb Lakewood Ranch – Lakewood Ranch, FL

Located in beautiful Lakewood Ranch about halfway between Bradenton and Sarasota, Del Webb Lakewood Ranch plans to accommodate 1,300 attached and single-family homes across 17,500 acres of land. Residents here will enjoy access to all of the resort-style amenities you might expect from a larger master-planned community.

Home options at Del Webb Lakewood Ranch include a 1,542 square foot attached villa or nine different single-family floor-plans that range from 1,289 to 2,634 square feet. Prices start in the $300k's.

delwebb.com/homes/florida/sarasota/lakewood-ranch/del-webb-lakewood-ranch-209449

Esplanade at Wiregrass Ranch - Wesley Chapel, FL

Esplanade at Wiregrass Ranch is a community of single-family homes located in Wesley Chapel with convenient access to downtown Tampa. It's an appealing combination of small-town charm and easy access to the big city.

You're never far from upscale retail shopping in the Shops at Wiregrass, highly-rated healthcare facilities, casual eateries, fine dining, professional sports, enticing entertainment and exciting Gulf Coast recreation.

Single family homes here range in size from about 1,700 to 3,500 sq. ft., and prices start in the $400k's.

taylormorrison.com/fl/tampa/wesley-chapel/esplanade-at-wiregrass-ranch

Manors at Angeline - Land O' Lakes, FL

The Manors is a collection of new single-family homes exclusively for active adults 55 and better at the Angeline master-plan community in Land O' Lakes, FL.

Residents will enjoy a private amenity center and clubhouse with a resort-style pool, fitness center and multiple sports courts. Spanning 6,200+ acres, Angeline will include a 750-acre Moffitt life sciences research park, community farm, up to 100 miles of trails and paved pathways, 3,600 acres of green space, Pasco County park, a MetroLagoon, and more.

Homes range in size from about 1,600 to 2,300 sq. ft. of living space and start in the $300k's.

lennar.com/new-homes/florida/tampa/land-o-lakes/angeline/manors

Mirada – San Antonio, FL

Mirada is a gated community of 858 attached and single-family homes in San Antonio, Florida. Residents here have access to their own private amenities like a community clubhouse, fitness center, and resort-style pool. Then they can also enjoy the impressive selection of amenities in the larger Mirada community.

Mirada offers attached homes that range in size from 1,396 to 1,731 square feet. The single-family homes start at 1,683 square feet and can get as big as 2,775 square feet. Prices start in the high $200k's.

lennar.com/new-homes/florida/tampa/san-antonio/mirada

Southshore Bay – Wimauma, FL

Southshore Bay is a community of 655 attached villas and single-family homes that is located in Wimauma, between Tampa and Bradenton. Available amenities here include a community clubhouse, fitness center, outdoor pool, and a large lagoon.

Southshore Bay offers villas and single-family homes that range in size from 1,396 to 2,775 square feet. Prices start in the $300k's.

lennar.com/new-homes/florida/tampa/wimauma/southshore-bay

Villages of Citrus Hills

Located just 10-minutes from the Gulf of Mexico (The Nature Coast), Citrus Hills residents get to enjoy endless outdoor recreation year-round, as well as resort-style country club amenities within the community gates. If you're interested in a diverse lifestyle with unique experiences and rolling hills, Citrus Hills just might be what you are looking for.

Citrus Hills offers offer a gated 55 plus neighborhood, as well as other neighborhood options that have no age restrictions for your Florida Retirement. Prices start in the $400k's.

citrushills.com

CENTRAL FLORIDA

This part of Florida is best known as a tourist destination because most of the theme parks in the state are located in Central Florida. Some prominent cities include Orlando, Lake Mary, Altamonte Springs, Winter Park, Kissimmee, Leesburg, Ocala, Gainesville, and Lakeland. The Villages, which is the most popular retirement community in the country is also located in Central Florida, about an hour north of Orlando.

Clermont

Sitting right in the heart of Central Florida, just 20 miles west of Orlando, is where you will find the impressive little city of Clermont, Florida. In the past it has at times been ranked as one of the Top 25 Best Places to Retire by Forbes and Money

Magazines and was also voted the #1 Florida Bicycle-Friendly Community.

As if that wasn't enough already, Clermont is also home to 18 athletes that competed in the 2016 Olympics, it is considered the center point of the impressive Coast-to-Coast Trail, and the city is still growing and developing at an incredible rate.

You can observe plenty of Clermont's rich history by simply strolling through the historic downtown area. It is here that you will find the iconic Florida Citrus tower. This famous landmark stands 226 feet tall and was constructed back in 1956.

There are also a number of outdoor attractions like Lake Louisa State Park, Crooked River Preserve, and Lake Minneola that each offer slightly different ways to experience and enjoy the great outdoors.

History is a big part of the culture in Clermont, so attractions like the Historic Village and the Presidents Hall of Fame are very popular locally. The Clermont Historic Villages offers a window into life in the area more than 100 years ago, and the Presidents Hall of Fame features wax statues of every president, as well as scale models of the White House, the Lincoln Memorial, and Mount Rushmore.

For the performing arts, there is the Clermont Performing Arts Center. Here you will find a wide range of plays, musicals, and other interesting events. The complex includes a 1,200 seat main stage and a smaller 250 seat venue as well.

With plenty of nearby communities to choose from, as well as lots of interesting things to do and amazing places to eat, it's easy to see why Clermont is a popular choice among retirees looking to enjoy themselves. Like the city motto says, Clermont is the "Choice of Champions."

Lake Nona

Located just inside the city limits in southeastern Orlando, Lake Nona is the ultimate combination of everything that most people are looking for in a retirement destination. The entire community is built around living a better, healthier lifestyle.

That means that residents here can enjoy an impressive amount of preserved green space, pools in every neighborhood, endless miles of trails, and some of the fastest internet speeds you will find anywhere in the world. On top of that, Lake Nona offers a plethora of educational options and outstanding healthcare facilities.

Lake Nona is a master-planned community that spans 7,000 acres. The area has been developed to include Lake Nona Medical City, which is a hub for biomedical research and education that features five difference medical facilities including a University of Central Florida College of Medicine and Health Sciences campus, the Sanford-Burnham Medical Research Institute, the Orlando VA Medical Center, Nemours Children's Hospital, and a University of Florida Research and Academic Center.

In addition to those fabulous medical facilities, Lake Nona also contains its own school system and five different neighborhoods that each offer a slightly different version of the Florida lifestyle you have been dreaming about.

Much of the community revolves around the Medical City, so Lake Nona is known for promoting healthy living among all of its residents. A full 40% of the community is dedicated to green spaces that include dog parks, athletic parks, playgrounds, and gardens. On top of that, there are resort-style and Olympic swimming pool options in each of the five neighborhoods.

Lake Nona residents also have access to state-of-the-art fitness centers located in each of the community neighborhoods, and there is a total of 44 miles of trails for walking or biking that crisscross throughout the community.

The United States Tennis Association has a state-of-the-art facility in Lake Nona, with 100 courts that houses the USTA's Community Tennis and Player Development divisions as well as the University of Central Florida's tennis teams. This facility is divided into dedicated areas that focus on the pathway from the youngest players to recreational players, to collegians, to future professional players and professional tour-level players.

It only takes one look at "The Beacon and Code Wall" at Lake Nona's Town Center to realize that this is a community where arts and culture play a pivotal role. This stunning artistic tribute looks spectacular against the night sky, while the much simpler "Glass House" is a beautiful artistic feature to visit during the day.

In addition to the culture you will find right in Lake Nona, residents are also close enough to enjoy all of the culture that Orlando has to offer, including the Dr. Phillips Center for the Performing Arts, the Orlando Philharmonic Orchestra, and the Orlando Ballet.

From the lifestyle and culture to the shopping and dining, everything about Lake Nona is built around the idea of emphasizing a healthier life that is filled with passion. If healthy living is something you are passionate about, this is definitely one place that should be on your list.

Ocala

The Ocala area represents a unique combination of history, horses, and culture that is surrounded by some of the most beautiful natural environments you will find anywhere. Sprinkle in the collection of interesting shops and restaurants in Ocala's downtown district and you will find Ocala to be the type of place where no one struggles to find something to do!

The early history of Ocala can be summed up in one word: rebuilding. The earliest inhabitants were the Timucua Indians, who abandoned their settlement after being attacked by explorer Hernando de Soto. The area would then be inhabited by Seminole Indians before the US Army built Fort King near Ocala.

As settlers began to build a new community around the base, many plantations were built in order to take advantage of the optimal citrus growing conditions. On Thanksgiving Day in 1883, the entire downtown district was leveled by a fire and Ocala residents were forced to rebuild the town once again.

The 1900's saw Ocala evolve into the "Horse Capital of the World" when Rosemere Farm and Bonnie Heath Farm both began producing some of the best thoroughbred horses in the world. To this day, Ocala remains one of the world's leading producers of thoroughbred horses. The 3,000 acre World Equestrian Center opened in 2021, with 1,500 permanent stalls, 4 indoor arenas, 17 outdoor arenas, and a 3-acre Grand Outdoor Stadium, a luxury hotel, RV sites and a variety of lifestyle amenities.

The headquarters of culture in Ocala is the Appleton Museum of Art. This fantastic marble structure was donated to the Ocala community by Arthur I. Appleton, who was a very successful horse breeder. The museum originally contained Appleton's personal collection but has grown by leaps and bounds over the years to become one of the foremost art museums in the state of Florida.

Another thing that the Ocala community is known for is leading an active lifestyle. Horses are still a huge business in the area, and there are a number of businesses that capitalize on this by offering horseback riding lessons and trail rides. In addition to horseback riding trails, the entire area is also surrounded by miles upon miles of hiking and paddling trails.

Downtown Ocala is best known for being an interesting collection of unique shops that sell everything from hand-made soaps to delicious baked goods. There is also a Farmer's Market held in downtown Ocala every Saturday from 9:00 am to 2:00 pm.

Whether you prefer the cultural aspect of the community, the active lifestyle opportunities, the one-of-a-kind shopping experience, or the great food, there is something for everyone in Ocala.

Ocala has long been known as "The Horse Capital of the World," but as the community has grown and evolved, that name no longer does the city justice. Visit and you'll soon discover Ocala area has far more to offer its residents and visitors.

Orlando

Everyone knows that Orlando is the theme park capital of the world, but there is a lot more to this beautiful city than those popular vacation destinations. Local residents enjoy a wide variety of outdoor activities, cultural attractions, excellent shopping, and delicious restaurants.

Of course, residents of Orlando also have the added perk of being able to visit all of the popular theme parks like Walt Disney World, Universal Orlando, and Sea World Orlando. But that is just the icing on the cake when you factor in all of the great things that Orlando has to offer!

Originally populated by Seminole Indians, the town of Orlando was officially incorporated just after the Civil War.

During that time, the area became the hub of the booming Florida citrus industry.

The most famous event in Orlando history happened in 1965 when Walt Disney announced his intentions to open Walt Disney World. After the resort opened in 1971, the tourism industry boomed along with the population and the local economy.

Tourism is a way of life in Orlando, and that translates into all kinds of fun activities and attractions for local residents to enjoy throughout the year. Orlando is also a golfer's paradise with more than 150 local courses to choose from.

The arts are also alive and well here in Orlando with enthralling performances taking center stage at the Dr. Phillips Center for the Performing Arts and breathtaking exhibits to explore at the Orlando Museum of Art and the Cornell Fine Arts Museum.

St. Cloud

Located along the southern banks of East Lake Tohopekaliga near Kissimmee and just south of Orlando, St. Cloud is a quiet city that was originally known as a retirement destination for Civil War veterans.

In addition to having a rich history, the area also offers a type of small-town living that is getting harder and harder to find here in Florida. Combining that small town atmosphere with access to all of the amazing amenities located just to the north in Orlando makes St. Cloud a perfect mixture of old and new Florida living.

Everything about the lifestyle in St. Cloud revolves around the community's small-town atmosphere. Whether you are looking to get out and enjoy the nearby lakes or keep to yourself on your private lanai, everything is calm in this town.

Because everything in St. Cloud is focused on small-town living, you aren't going to find a massive cultural community here. However, you can easily make up for that by heading right up the road to Kissimmee or Orlando.

The Villages

Golf carts lined up in The Villages

Located about an hour north of Orlando, The Villages was not even called "The Villages" when it first began. It started as a mobile home park called Orange Blossom Gardens. Though it struggled in the early years, the community experienced staggering growth in the mid-1980's because the community offered an impressive collection of amenities.

As that amenities-focused community continued to grow and develop, it eventually evolved into The Villages, which has become the premiere model for what a master-planned community should be.

Today, The Villages is known for having the largest and most diverse collection of amenities of any community on the planet. Residents have access to an amazing collection of golf courses, recreation centers, and town squares, as well as an unparalleled number of clubs covering just about any topic you can imagine.

With all of the advantages that The Villages offers to its residents, it is no wonder that it consistently ranks as one of the fastest growing communities in the entire country. There were an astounding 4,004 new homes sold here in 2021.

Set foot in The Villages for the first time and you will instantly note that just about everyone here uses a golf cart for their day-to-day travels. Almost everywhere you need or want to go in The Villages is golf cart accessible, which makes getting around much simpler.

There are several golf cart dealerships and service centers throughout The Villages and there are also regularly scheduled golf cart safety clinics which are great for newcomers.

The Villages has more holes of golf than any other community/facility in the world and at the time of this writing in 2022 there are 711 holes of golf in The Villages spread across 42 Executive Courses and 12 Championship Courses.

In addition to great golfing, The Villages also contains a large number of tennis courts. There are courts available at most of the recreation centers, and there are also three larger tennis centers located throughout the community.

There is a whole lot more to life in The Villages than just golf and tennis! The Villages is a great place for pickleball, which is one of the fastest growing sports in the country. There are also active softball leagues, and if you want to try something new, Dragonboat Racing is very popular.

If active competition isn't your thing, that's fine too. There are more than 3,000 different clubs and organizations that cover topics ranging from woodworking to watercolor painting to scrabble to political debates.

Residents here also have plenty of opportunities to hit one of the town squares or various other commercial areas for great dining, fantastic shopping, and plenty of fun entertainment.

Depending on your location in The Villages, you might prefer the Santa Fe plaza feel of Spanish Springs Town Square, the beautiful lake views at Lake Sumter Landing Market Square, or the rustic feel of Brownwood Paddock Square. Each of these town squares contains great restaurants and shops.

There is free nightly entertainment in the town squares, but ticketed shows and performances regularly take place in The Villages at the Savannah Center and The Sharon Morse Performing Arts Center.

The best way to see what The Villages is all about is to visit it yourself. For doing that, you've got several options. The "official" way for prospective buyers to visit is to take part in The Villages Lifestyle Preview Program.

The Villages Lifestyle Preview allows prospective residents the opportunity to come live like a Villager for anywhere from 4 to 7 days. For longer stays, you could find a rental. Some people opt totally out of buying altogether, and just rent here for several months a year.

This overview of The Villages just barely scratches the surface of all of the information you are going to want to consider before making the decision to pick up and move here. There is an incredible amount of information you are going to want to know about The Villages that goes well beyond the scope of these last few pages.

The next step in continuing your education about The Villages is to order and read through my book, **Inside the Bubble: Unauthorized Guide to Florida's Most Popular Community**, which covers all of these topics in much greater detail.

insidethebubble.net/book/

Winter Garden

Located about 25 minutes west of downtown Orlando, Winter Garden offers residents the perfect combination of an Old Florida feel and plenty of modern amenities. You'll love strolling through the historic downtown district but will also enjoy the lake lifestyle, the thriving cultural scene, shopping at the weekly farmers' market, and dining at the impressive collection of modern restaurants.

After just over 50 years of settlers moving to the area along Lake Apopka, the modern history of Winter Garden started when the city was officially established in 1903 and incorporated in 1908.

The new lakeside community grew quickly during the roaring 20's, but that growth slowed considerably during the 1960s due in part to the pollution of Lake Apopka. Things started to pick up again in the 1970s, and the area has seen tremendous growth in the years that followed.

After placing its downtown district on the National Register of Historic Places in 1996, Winter Garden has evolved as a model for combining a rich history with modern amenities.

The lifestyle in Winter Garden has always revolved around embracing the benefits of living along the banks of Lake Apopka, which is still in the process of being restored but has seen significant water quality improvements. Whether you are interested in boating, fishing, swimming, or kayaking, there is something for everyone to enjoy out on the lake.

Winter Garden is also one of the stops on the West Orange Trail, which is a part of the massive 250-mile Coast-to-Coast Connector Trail that runs across Central Florida. This makes it an ideal location for cycling enthusiasts.

Whether you are passionate about life on the lake, excited to dig into the local restaurant options, or just want to be close to Orlando without feeling overwhelmed by tourists, Winter

Garden is a perfect retirement destination for anyone looking for Old Florida charm matched with modern amenities.

CENTRAL FLORIDA COMMUNITIES

Note: On my website I've got a handy list of all the communities mentioned in this book at: floridaforboomers.com/list

Covered Bridge – Lake Placid, FL

Located about two hours south of Orlando in Lake Placid, Covered Bridge is a community of 230 attached and single-family homes. Residents here enjoy access to amenities like a community clubhouse, heated pool, and a community boat ramp.

New single-family homes are available in eight different ranch-style floorplans that range in size from about 1,000 square feet to a little over 1,400 square feet. Prices start in the $200k's.

coveredbridgelakeplacid.com

Del Webb Mineola - Mineola

Del Webb Mineola is a new 55+ community scheduled to open soon just north of Clermont. The community is only one mile from the Florida Turnpike, which makes getting just about anywhere you need to go in the greater Orlando area extremely easy. You can expect to see the same types of homes and amenities offered in other Del Webb communities here in Florida.

delwebb.com/homes/florida/orlando/minneola/del-webb-minneola-210777

Del Webb Oasis – Winter Garden, FL

Del Webb Oasis is a new community in the heart of Central Florida offering both single-family homes and villas.

The main difference between all of the Del Webb communities in Florida is their location, and this one is pretty unique in that it is just minutes from Disney. Del Webb Oasis is slated to include a 14,000 square foot clubhouse that will be situated to provide an excellent view of theme park fireworks.

Del Webb Oasis offers single-family homes and villas. Prices start in the $400k's.

delwebb.com/homes/florida/orlando/winter-garden/del-webb-oasis-210212

Del Webb Stone Creek – Ocala, FL

Del Webb Stone Creek is a gated, 55+ active adult community located in the horse capital of the world, Ocala, FL. One of the only new Del Webb's in Florida with an 18-hole championship golf course, there's also a full grill/restaurant, resort-style pool, fitness center, spa, multiple game courts, a full-time lifestyle director and more. Prices start in the $200k's.

delwebb.com/homes/florida/tampa/ocala/del-webb-stone-creek-12357

Del Webb Sunbridge – St. Cloud, FL

Del Webb Sunbridge is a new 55+ gated community in St. Cloud, which is in Central Florida, just minutes from Lake Nona and Orlando.

The 27,000 sf. Clubhouse features luxurious indoor and outdoor amenities like a zero-entry pool, resistance pool, pickleball and tennis courts, a fitness center, movement studio, and more.

Both single-family homes and villas are available. Prices start in the high $300k's.

delwebb.com/homes/florida/orlando/st-cloud/del-webb-sunbridge-210031

Four Seasons at Orlando – Kissimmee, FL

Four Seasons at Orlando is a gated community of 557 single-family homes that is located in Kissimmee, Florida, just south of Orlando. Amenities here include a 14,000 square foot clubhouse with a state-of-the-art fitness center and an arts and crafts room, as well as an outdoor swimming pool, pickleball courts, and access to the 18-hole Mystic Dunes Golf Club.

There are 7 floorplans that range in size from 1,428 to 2,328 square feet. Prices start in the $300k's.

khov.com/find-new-homes/florida/kissimmee/34747/four-seasons/k.-hovnanian's-four-seasons-at-orlando

Gatherings of Lake Nona – Orlando, FL

Gatherings of Lake Nona is a community of 216 condos located inside the master-planned community of Lake Nona, just outside of Orlando. Residents here can enjoy a low-maintenance lifestyle, as well as access to amenities like a large clubhouse, outdoor pool, and a dog park.

The condos at Gatherings of Lake Nona are available in four different floor plans offer two or three bedrooms. Those condos can be as small as 1,368 square feet, and they can be as large as 1,805 square feet. Prices start in the $400k's.

beazer.com/orlando-fl/gatherings-of-lake-nona

JB Ranch – Ocala, FL

With construction that just started in 2017, JB Ranch is one of the newer communities in the Ocala area. Plans here call for a total of 346 single-family homes, and the list of amenities includes a community clubhouse, fitness center, and outdoor pool with patio seating.

Homes range in size from 1,641 to 2,034 square feet. Prices start in the $300k's.

drhorton.com/florida/west-central-florida/ocala/freedom-jb-ranch

Lake Ashton - Winter Haven, FL

Set on over 1,200 scenic acres, amongst three spectacular lakes and nature preserves, Lake Ashton offers a great retirement lifestyle in the heart of Florida. This award winning, 24-hour manned gated community is tucked between Tampa and Orlando.

Lake Ashton has two 18-hole golf courses, a 26,000 sq. ft. main clubhouse, a 30,000 sq. ft. fitness center, community pools, pickleball and tennis courts, and so much more.

New homes and resales are available from the $300k's.

lakeashton.com/

Lake James – Lakeland, FL

Lake James is a low-maintenance community of 216 single-family homes that is located right outside of Lakeland. Amenities here include a 2,000 square foot clubhouse with a fitness room and a resort-style outdoor pool, as well as miles of walking and hiking trails.

The homes at Lake James are available in more than a dozen different layouts ranging from as small as 1,510 square feet to a much larger 2,420 square feet.

lakejamesadultcommunity.com

Lakes of Mount Dora – Mount Dora, FL

Located just north of Orlando, Lakes of Mount Dora is a gated community of 950 single-family homes that combines 178 acres of lakes with New England-style architecture. Amenities here include an 18,000 square foot clubhouse complete with a fitness center and a banquet facility. Then there is the resort-style pool and hot tub outside.

Lakes of Mount Dora offers a few different ranch-style homes that range in size from as small as 1,263 square feet all the way up to something as large as 3,700 square feet. Prices start in the $400k's.

medallionhome.com/communities/lakes-of-mount-dora/

Liberty Village - Ocala

Liberty Village is a masterplan community of new homes exclusively for residents aged 55 and better in Ocala. The community is surrounded by beautiful lakes and a rolling countryside filled with gorgeous thoroughbred horse farms. The community features proximity to great shopping and dining options at historic Downtown Ocala, as well as popular hot spots for water sports, including Silver Glen Springs, Rainbow Springs State Park and the Crystal Springs of Ocala.

Homes range in size from about 1,500 to 2,200 sq. Ft. Of living area and start in the $300k's.

lennar.com/new-homes/florida/ocala/ocala/liberty-village

Ocala Preserve - Ocala, FL

Ocala Preserve is a 623-acre community of 1,600 single-family homes located in Marion County, Florida. Amenities here include a 17,000 square foot clubhouse with a state-of-the-art fitness center, a zero-entry resort-style pool, and an 18-hole championship golf course.

New homes at Ocala Preserve are available in a variety of different collections that range in size from as small as 1,320 square feet up to 2,370 square feet. Prices start in the $200k's.

sheahomes.com/new-homes/florida/central-flor-ida/ocala/ocala-preserve/

On Top of the World – Ocala, FL

At On Top of the World, active adults will find all they dream about and so much more. Located in beautiful Ocala Florida, On Top of the World residents can enjoy any schedule that suits their tastes – from activity packed to unhurried.

Leisure amenities include 54 holes of golf on three courses, indoor and outdoor swimming pools, tennis courts, a 14-acre R/C flying field, bocce, racquetball and basketball courts, fitness center, health club and spa, restaurants, cultural venues, and much more.

Residents can also participate in over 175 clubs, leagues, hobbies, and lifelong learning opportunities.

There are 23 different floor plans available. Prices start in the $200k's.

ontopoftheworldcommunities.com

Palms at Serenoa – Clermont, FL

Located just west of Orlando, Palms at Serenoa is a gated community of 570 attached villas and single-family homes that began construction in 2018. Residents here enjoy access to amenities like a community clubhouse, fitness center, resort-style pool, and more than 16 acres of parks and green spaces around the community.

The attached homes at Palms at Serenoa are a 1,608 square foot floorplan with two bedrooms and two bathrooms. The single-family homes range in size from 1,402 to 2,034 square feet and come in six different models. Prices start in the $300k's.

drhorton.com/florida/central-florida/clermont/freedom-serenoa

Solivita - Kissimmee, FL

Solivita is a national award-winning retirement community in Central Florida's attraction zone, offering great natural beauty, vast recreational amenities and enough to do to keep any active adult as busy as you care to be. No matter where you live within this lush gated 55-plus community in Kissimmee, you can easily walk, bike or drive your golf cart to indoor and outdoor dining venues, state-of-the-art spa and fitness complexes, pickleball or tennis courts, and other facilities for sports and games.

With two stunning championship golf courses, intimate neighborhood centers, softball field, miles of green space for walking, cycling and meandering, and too many classes and clubs to count, you will have many ways to enjoy the Solivita life. Residents have access to a full-time on-site Activities Director and Lifestyle Team dedicated to creating a diverse, packed schedule of events, as well as assisting the 200+ Social Clubs created by Solivita residents. Prices start in the $200k's.

taylormorrison.com/fl/orlando/kissimmee/solivita

Stonecrest - Summerfield, FL

Stonecrest is a 55+ community that has been around for decades, and Lennar is building the last few homes here. Amenities here include an 18-hole golf course, a family-friendly pool and more. Residents also enjoy easy access to great shopping and dining options nearby, including in The Villages which is just minutes away.

Home sizes range from about 1,700 sq. ft. to more than 2,300 sq. ft. Prices start in the $300k's.

lennar.com/new-homes/florida/ocala/summerfield/stonecrest

The Lakes at Harmony – St. Cloud, FL

The Lakes at Harmony offers two and three bedroom homes built for the way retirees live, with space where they need it most. Residents here enjoy less crowded living with spacious outdoor living areas, many of which include water or conservation views, and a private recreation center and pool.

From the miles of walking and biking trails, to the community garden, parks and fitness center, Harmony has something for everyone. Gather at the Town Square which includes a spa, market, physician office, restaurants and more or play a round of golf on the only Johnny Miller Signature course in Central Florida without ever leaving your community. Prices start in the $400k's.

joneshomesusa.com/lakes-at-harmony

The Villages - The Villages, FL

The Villages is one of the largest active adult communities in the entire world. With three different town squares, more than 35 community centers, more than 80 different pools, and more than 50 different golf courses, the list of amenities available to "Villagers" as residents are affectionately known goes on for days.

Just like the list of amenities, the list of floorplans available around The Villages is massive. You can pretty much find anything your heart desires in Florida's most-popular retirement community. Homes here start out in the $200k's, but there are also plenty of high-end options with prices ranging all the way up into the $1 million-plus range.

thevillages.com

Note: I have another book dedicated solely to The Villages titled "Inside the Bubble". You can learn more at: insidethebubble.net/book/

Tohoqua Reserve - Kissimmee

Tohoqua Reserve is a 55+ Active Adult neighborhood from Pulte Homes. It is located within a master planned community in Kissimmee. Tohoqua Reserve is less than 10 minutes from the Florida Turnpike, making commutes to all major areas of Orlando much easier.

Amenities include a private amenity center exclusively reserved for active adults with a clubhouse, resort-style pool, sports courts, and more.

Single family homes and villas are available in sizes ranging from 1,500 sq. ft. to more than 2,800 sq. ft. Prices start in the $300k's.

pulte.com/homes/florida/orlando/kissimmee/tohoqua-reserve-210549

Twin Lakes – St. Cloud, FL

Residents of Twin Lakes can enjoy lakeside living with boating, fishing, kayaking and many other amenities.

With a clubhouse, pool, patio areas, newly opened fitness center and a full-time activities director, there is something for everyone in this outstanding community. Twin Lakes, by Jones Homes USA, is now selling new homes with luxury features and advanced home technology, in the "convenient to everything," Orlando Area. Prices start in the $400k's.

joneshomesusa.com/twin-lakes

CHAPTER THIRTEEN
HOA'S, CDD'S, AND BEYOND

IN THIS CHAPTER I'm going to cover a handful of topics that will be nearly unavoidable for most people moving to Florida. These include Homeowners Associations, Condo Associations, Community Development Districts, and the fees that can be associated with each.

Homeowners Associations

The general idea behind a homeowners association (HOA) is that you have a group of people elected by the residents who make up the board directing the homeowners association. The main duties are to 1) represent the best interests of the residents of the community especially in the capacity of protecting home values through the implementation and enforcement of rules, known as covenants and restrictions and 2) to assess and collect homeowners' fees to help pay for the upkeep of common areas of the community as well as any other areas provided for in the covenants and deed recordings.

HOA Fees and Dues

Homeowners' association dues vary widely depending on the amount of amenities that are provided to the homeowners. Some just cover the maintenance of the common areas including medians, right of ways, lakes, and ponds. Other dues can cover things such as upkeep of the streets (if they are private streets), and streetlights. Some communities negotiate for a group rate on cable TV or Internet access with service providers. You may be charged fees for those services monthly, quarterly, or yearly. Failure to pay your homeowner's dues can result in the association placing a lien on your property and eventually foreclosing if you get far enough behind on your payments.

As a prospective purchaser in a community, you are entitled to and encouraged to review the budget. When deciding whether a homeowners' association's dues are a good deal or not, add up what you think it would cost you to obtain the services provided on your own. Don't forget the aggravation the association saves you by not having to deal with finding and scheduling the services and vendors yourself.

If you are buying a home in a new subdivision where homes are still under construction, odds are that the developer still controls the homeowners' association. Until control of the HOA is given to the resident owners, called turnover, which the state of Florida requires to occur when 90% of the units in a community have sold and closed, the developer is still responsible for maintaining the public aspects of the community (streets, common areas, etc.) and carrying out the duties of creating a budget for the Association and setting HOA dues accordingly.

Oftentimes the developer will over-subsidize the budget, in order to keep the initial HOA fees low, in an effort to attract more buyers. But when turnover occurs, and the developer is no longer subsidizing the budget, homeowners can be hit with a sharp increase in their HOA dues. Before purchasing in a community where the developer controls the HOA, make sure that you carefully review the budget to make sure everyone is paying their fair share, or if that is not the case, try to reasonably figure out what your dues might be when control of the development turns over.

When looking at communities here in Florida you'll see HOA fees that may seem low and some that may seem high. Some people have a tendency to compare the fees at various communities and unfairly conclude that the communities with the lowest fees are "a better deal".

This is not always the case! More times than not, when you see a community with higher fees, the fee includes more services and amenities. Most of the time these end up being things you would pay for on your own anyway.

For example, a community with a $100/month HOA fee might include use of a community pool, tennis/pickleball courts, common area maintenance, and upkeep/maintenance of an electronic gate, while a community with a $500/month HOA fee might include all of that PLUS exterior landscape maintenance at your house (mowing, trimming of shrubs, mulching, irrigation maintenance, etc.), a 24-hour manned guard/gatehouse, fitness center, a full-time activities director, organized social activities, cable TV, internet, house painting and pressure washing, and more.

You really have to look at what each community includes in their fees and try to compare apples to apples. This is one of the main reasons most communities don't list all of their fees on their websites for all to see. They'd rather have one of their trained salespeople explain the fees to you, describing exactly what they include for the money.

What you also need to understand is that, with very few exceptions, these fees are NOT designed to be profit centers. There's not some wizard behind the curtain getting rich off of the fees and dues you're paying to live wherever you decide to live.

Common HOA Rules and Regulations

Another aspect of communities with homeowners' associations is that most involve rules and regulations, or covenants and restrictions (C and Rs) also referred to as covenants, conditions, and restrictions (C, C and Rs). Be sure to ask for a copy before you sign any purchase agreement, and make sure that the agreement is contingent on (depends upon) your understanding and approval of the covenants and restrictions and rules and regulations.

Some common rules and regulations that may be included in the documents are rules regarding:

Fences

Some communities have restrictions on what type of fence you may have, the material it can be made of, how high it can be, or if any fences are allowed at all. If a community you are considering does not allow fences at all, and you have pets that require being fenced in, you might have to consider an invisible fence.

Parking

Overnight or long-term street parking are often not allowed. This is as much a fire and police safety issue as it is an aesthetic issue. Boats and trailers are usually not allowed to be stored outside, so you must find room in your garage or park them offsite.

Changes to the exterior of your home

Most homeowners' associations require that an architectural or design review committee approve any changes you wish to make to the exterior of your home. This includes things such as adding a screened-in patio, swimming pool, or painting your home a different color. Even changes to your land-scaping must sometimes be approved.

There is usually a form they have you fill out on which you must describe in detail any changes you plan to make, including a list of materials to be used, who will do the work, and so on. You are also typically required to submit any draw-ings or plans that show how the change will look when complete. This is to keep everything in the neighborhood looking nice and congruent.

Pets

Some communities have restrictions on the number of pets you may have in a home. Size restrictions are also common in condominiums or apartments, though I have seen some single family home communities with size restrictions as well, so always be sure to ask what the rules are if you own a pet.

Some communities may have you register your pets and show proof that they've had their shots, particularly if there is a dog park in the community where they could be interacting closely with other dogs.

Here's how one Del Webb community I recently reviewed as part of my Florida Retirement Insider Membership spells out their pet rules:

1. Owners must register pets with the Association and are granted a license to maintain not more than three (3) pets per Lot. Pets must be contained or on a short leash [less than 15 feet] when they are outside of the dwelling unit. Pets must be contained or on a short leash no greater than Six (6) feet on any portion of the Common Areas. Owners are responsible for the activities of its pet(s) and are required to pick up, remove and properly dispose of litter deposited by their pet(s) on the Common Areas throughout the community.

2. No pet or animal is allowed in amenity buildings or on property surrounding the amenity buildings, unless the pet or animal is a service animal. No pet

or animal shall be "tied out" or left unattended on any Common Areas, or in the Common Areas. Pets that would be considered dangerous by the Board of Directors will not be permitted.

Again, the rules will vary by community. I've just included this here as an example of the kinds of rules you might see.

Protection of home values

It can sound like a pain to have to pay all of these fees and abide by these restrictions especially if you are coming from a community that doesn't have any fees or restrictions. But all these fees and rules, as inconvenient as they may sometimes seem, do serve the important purpose of protecting your home values. If you are going to pay a quarter of a million dollars or more for your new home here in Florida, you want to know that someone is looking out for you and your investment. Ask any reputable real estate agent or property appraiser and they will tell you that communities governed by homeowners' associations have the best track record of preserving and increasing home values.

Deciding if an HOA is for you

So, based on this information, do you think a community with a homeowners' association is for you? If you're at all like me, the answer is a resounding yes. I like knowing that my best interests are being looked after and my home value is being protected. You basically just have to weigh out the pros and cons of living in such a structured environment. While it's not for everybody, I think that most people will ultimately choose to live in and be happy in communities with a home-owners' association. I think it's best for your lifestyle and the future value of your property.

Condominium Associations and Related Fees

Some of you will end up in a condominium. As an owner of a condo you will be responsible for paying condo fees. Before buying a condo, make sure these fees have been explained to you in writing. You should also ask to see the budget. When buying a resale condo in Florida you have a three-day "cooling off" period (7 days for new condo construction) during which you may ask to cancel your contract. This is so that potential condo buyers have ample opportunity to examine and understand the condo fees, rules, and budget. Remember though that this only applies to condos, the same "cooling off" period does not apply to any other type of property.

The condo fees are collected to pay for things like mainte-nance of the exterior of the condo, including insurance on the building, maintenance of the common areas, such as the grounds, swimming pool, and other amenities. Quite frequently in a condo the condo fee includes water, sewer, and garbage service. This is often more convenient for you: almost no one complains about having a few less checks to write each and every month.

Special Assessments

Eventually, if you live in a condo (and even with a homeown-ers' association) long enough, you may fall prey to what is called a special assessment. A special assessment is sometimes a necessary evil and is used to pay for items such as a new roof or unexpected repairs beyond ordinary maintenance. Your association's budget should have a reserve set aside for unexpected events, but sometimes if there is not enough money to pay for what needs to be done, unit owners will be assessed. If you are on a shoestring budget or have a fixed income with little reserves, you may want to rethink a condo because just one special assessment can put you in the red.

Also note that failure to pay any of your condo fees or special assessments can result in the condo association placing a lien on your property, which can eventually lead to foreclosure.

Community Development Districts

Some popular communities you look at in Florida will be part of what are called Community Development Districts (CDD). A CDD is a special purpose government framework permitted by Florida Statutes and used by local governments and developers to shift the burden of developing infrastructure, maintaining roads and landscaping, building clubhouses, and other improvements to the homeowners in that district or area.

The general idea with a CDD is that you shift the burden of paying for infrastructure and development from the developer to those who directly benefit, which typically means homeowners in those newly developed areas.

The way they work is the CDD run by a board that is chosen by the developer issues bonds to pay for the infrastructure and other community improvements.

In the early days of a development, since the developer is the primary landowner this makes sense, but once a certain percentage of homes are sold control over the decision-making process shifts to the actual homeowners.

The massive costs of building the infrastructure are financed by the developer with a key CDD incentive, which is tax-free municipal bonds.

What's Included in a CDD Fee?

- water management and control
- water supply
- sewer
- wastewater management
- bridges and culverts
- district roads and streetlights
- public transportation and parking
- investigation and remediation of environmental contamination
- conservation areas
- parks and recreation facilities
- fire prevention and control
- school buildings and related structures
- security
- waste collection and disposal
- mosquito control

Obviously not all CDD's will have each of those items, but most of these are quite common.

The amount homeowners are assessed for these is added to their tax bill. Rather than paying for everything up front when they buy their home, homeowners pay the ultimate costs for the infrastructure over a span of 15 to 30 years, but they also have to pay for the ongoing upkeep of that infrastructure for as long as they live in the district.

That's an important point a lot of people don't understand. They hear about people paying off their CDD bond and they think that's it, but no, there will always be a CDD maintenance fee to cover the cost of maintaining everything.

The Downsides of CDD's

CDD's can go bad, and many did during the 2007-2009 recession. CDD's have gone bankrupt in Florida. This is just another reason why it's vitally important that you find and work with an agent who really knows what's going on where you're thinking about buying. It's their duty to help point this kind of stuff out to you.

CDD financial problems can really only be helped in a few ways. One, an increase in demand for real estate within that district creates the needed revenue to cover bond payments. Or, as has happened in several instances, the bad debt along with the land and improvements on it are bought at such large discount that the new owners are able to go in and build the community and sell homes at prices that are attractive enough to generate a flood of new sales. But just because a certain area is in high demand, it doesn't necessarily mean their CDD's aren't at risk.

A perfect example of this is The Villages which is home to several CDD's. As you probably know, The Villages is the most popular retirement community in Florida.

The Villages CDD's have come under attack in the past by the IRS which had an investigation going on for several years looking into whether these CDDs have been controlled and run according to the rules that are in place to keep them tax exempt.

The probe ended in 2016.

What is the prospective retirement community home buyer to do? Do your homework and proceed with caution.

CDD's are not necessarily a bad thing as they can provide a community with amenities and services it otherwise might not get. You just have to be careful and know what you're getting yourself into before buying in a CDD.

There are new CDD's popping up all the time, so always be sure to ask when buying a home if it is in a CDD, and if so, learn as much as you can about the financial health and stability of that particular CDD.

Do CDD Fees Ever Go Away?

Remember that you will be required to pay both a CDD infrastructure assessment and a maintenance assessment.

The infrastructure assessment can be paid off and many homeowners choose to do that. You'll see some resales advertise with the statement, "no bond", or "bond paid". But you'll ALWAYS have the CDD maintenance assessment to contend with. That part will never go away.

How CDD Fees Are Calculated

Here's how the CDD infrastructure and maintenance assessments are calculated.

Now, you'll never have to do this calculation yourself, but I think it just helps to see how they come up with the numbers. For simplicity's sake we'll use some nice big round numbers.

Let's say the infrastructure construction costs $10 million, and there are a thousand acres within the district and the specific unit within the district your home is located in has 100 acres and there are 200 lots.

The math would be $10 million divided by 1000 acres, which equals $10,000 per acre. Remember, your unit has 100 acres at $10,000 per acre, or a million dollars for your unit. A million dollars divided by the 200 lots equals $5,000 bond per lot for your unit.

The annual CDD maintenance assessment is calculated in much the same way except it is based on the annual budget established by the board of supervisors for each district, rather than the one-time fixed infrastructure cost.

Whether you're working with a new home sales agent from the development or an outside realtor, they should be able to tell you what the current CDD assessments are due for each property you see.

Are CDD Fees Tax Deductible?

Now, as I said earlier, the amount you'll have to pay for the CDD will come on your property tax bill, which naturally begs the question are my CDD assessments deductible on my federal tax return?

Well, the IRS says that it is not deductible because it is an assessment not an ad valorem tax.

Lots of people just go ahead and deduct it because the check is made out to the tax collector for the entire amount. The tax collector keeps the taxes due and sends the remainder of the money to the CDD, but technically only a portion of that check is actually property taxes.

Do people go ahead and deduct the full amount and get away with it? I'm sure they probably do but they're not supposed to, and I'd strongly advise you against trying to stiff the IRS.

CHAPTER FOURTEEN
SAFEST PLACES

ACCORDING to the Florida Department of Law Enforcement, Florida's total crime rate has gone down by 60% since 1998.

It has never been safer to live in Florida than it is right now.

Each year, at least until the start of the Covid-19 pandemic (more on that in a minute), the FBI released crime data for the previous year for all Metropolitan Statistical Areas (MSA's) in the United States, including the 22 MSA's in Florida.

I thought it would be interesting to crunch their numbers and see which places in Florida may actually be the safest to live and retire in.

The FBI data is broken down into 9 different categories:

- Violent crime
- Murder and non-negligent manslaughter

- Rape
- Robbery
- Aggravated assault
- Property Crime
- Burglary
- Larceny-theft
- Motor vehicle theft

The data is most easily digested when distilled into a "Rate per 100,000 inhabitants".

So, to find the safest places to live and retire in Florida, we simply have to look at the areas with the lowest number of crime incidents (rate) per 100,000 inhabitants.

I feel it's important to note that Florida's crime figures have skewed lower since the Covid-19 pandemic, due in part to several months during which people were out and about much less, and also some inconsistencies in reporting from various agencies. To counter that, I've used numbers from the last full pre-pandemic year for this illustration.

Before we get to the numbers, keep in mind that a seemingly high crime rate for one M.S.A. does not mean the entire area is unsafe.

Crime tends to occur most frequently in the more densely populated areas, and most of the communities you'll be looking at for retirement are outside of those areas.

I think what you'll find that most 55+ communities are just as safe (or even safer due to lower populations) than even the "safest" M.S.A.'s as a whole.

For a number of reasons, the FBI cautions against using their data to compile rankings, so try not to consider what follows as "rankings" per se. Try to look at it as "I've just put them in order for you to make them easier to read".

The following data is listed as Metropolitan Statistical Area (MSA) followed by the number of Crimes Per 100,000 Inhabitants.

The Villages, FL M.S.A.: 2,089

Punta Gorda, FL M.S.A.: 2,653

Naples-Marco Island, FL M.S.A.: 2,715

Cape Coral-Fort Myers, FL M.S.A.: 2,831

Port St. Lucie, FL M.S.A.: 3,021

Sebastian-Vero Beach, FL M.S.A.: 3,081

Homosassa Springs, FL M.S.A.: 3,287

Lakeland-Winter Haven, FL M.S.A.: 3,845

Tampa-St. Petersburg-Clearwater, FL M.S.A.: 3,956

Crestview-Fort Walton Beach-Destin, FL M.S.A.: 3,966

North Port-Sarasota-Bradenton, FL M.S.A.: 4,005

Deltona-Daytona Beach-Ormond Beach, FL M.S.A.: 4,249

Ocala, FL M.S.A.: 4,651

Palm Bay-Melbourne-Titusville, FL M.S.A.: 4,835

Sebring-Avon Park, FL M.S.A.: 4,967

Pensacola-Ferry Pass-Brent, FL M.S.A.: 5,175

Orlando-Kissimmee-Sanford, FL M.S.A.: 5,660

Jacksonville, FL M.S.A.: 5,960

Miami-Fort Lauderdale-Pompano Beach, FL M.S.A.: 6,216

Gainesville, FL M.S.A.: 6,292

Tallahassee, FL M.S.A.: 6,916

Panama City, FL M.S.A.: 7,022

FLORIDA IS CONSISTENTLY RANKED one of the most tax-friendly states for retirement, as well as one of the most affordable states for retirement. But everyone's budget and financial situation is different, so I've put together this chapter to help you figure out what it might actually cost you to live in Florida.

Now, every city and community will be different, so I think the easiest way to go about this is to give you a complete cost of living breakdown for what is currently the most popular retirement community in the entire country, The Villages in Central Florida.

Yes, some places will be more expensive. Some places will be less expensive. But the point here is to give you a good idea of what you might have to pay for, not so much exactly what they cost.

It's important to keep in mind that many of these costs are not going to apply to everyone, I'm just trying to get it all down on paper and you can pick what's applicable and what's not. Two items noticeably absent are healthcare and health insurance. These vary so much from person to person, and I have no way of predicting what these would be for you, just be sure you include whatever you think your costs might be in your budget.

Last but not least, for any housing related costs, assume the figures below are for a $350,000 home. Buying a million-dollar home in Florida? Your costs will undoubtedly be higher.

Mortgage payment

I know many people pay cash for their homes, but many choose to carry a mortgage, even if it's just for tax deduction reasons. If you visit Bankrate.com you can calculate this one using your own figures but I used a $350,000 house, with 20% down, and a 30-year fixed rate mortgage at 6% and came up with $1678 per month.

But again, a lot of people buying here in Florida do pay for their homes in cash and never get a mortgage, so a mortgage payment may or may not apply to you.

Homeowners Insurance

Insurance has gone up the last few years. You'll learn more about why in Chapter 19. For a $350,000 house in The Villages, $200 month is probably a good estimate. Of course you can adjust this up or down based on how much home you intend to buy accordingly, and every area will be different.

Also, even if because of where you are buying you won't be required to carry it, I always tell people to get flood insurance too just in case. So let's call that an additional $400/year or about $33/month to be safe.

Amenities Fee/HOA Fee

In The Villages, there is not an HOA per se, like you'll find in a lot of other communities. Instead, they have what they call an amenities fee. At $179 a month currently (changes tied to the CPI) this covers much of what makes The Villages such a draw. Things like golf on the executive courses, swimming, tennis, organized activities, 24-hour neighborhood watch and more.

Some communities will have a higher fee that includes more perks, and some communities will have a lower fee that includes much less. You get the idea.

Property Taxes

In addition to the value of the home, the actual amount you pay in taxes will depend on whether you qualify for homestead exemption, and which county the home is located in. But for a $350,000 home count on paying between $3,500 and $5,000 per year, which works out to between $291 and $416 per month.

Bond/CDD Assessments

This may or may not apply to you, depending on where you buy. Most people buying homes in The Villages have a CDD infrastructure assessment and a CDD maintenance assessment. The infrastructure assessment can be paid off, and many homeowners choose to do that. You'll see some resales advertised with the statement "Bond paid". But regardless you'll always have the CDD maintenance assessment to contend with.

These can range from below $100 to more than $500. Again, this is going to depend on what type of home you ultimately end up with, where it's located, if the bond is paid, and so on.

Utilities

In my opinion utilities are tough enough to estimate, let alone when you estimate them individually. You've got people that never set the thermostat below 80 thus they have a consistent power bill, but maybe they love their 30-minute showers leaving them with a higher water bill than others. So for simplicity's sake lets lump them into two groups.

For water, sewer, power, and trash collection in The Villages I'd estimate $300-$350 AND add another $100-$200 if you have a pool to cover the costs of running a pool pump. Add even more if you have an electric or gas pool heater.

Basic cable is estimated about $60, but that does not include phone and internet. Of course most companies will let you bundle cable, phone, and internet but if you do this, in my experience it will cost more than $60.

Some people may forgo a landline in lieu of using cell phones exclusively. But no matter which route you choose, I'd budget between $150 and $250 for phone, cable, and internet.

Landscaping

You might think cutting your own grass and trimming your trees and shrubs sounds like a good idea at first, but most people eventually agree it's either too dang hot or they are just too dang busy to keep up with it all. So most opt for a lawn service to come.

I'd estimate $75 $150/month for an average home. Of course it's going to depend on the size of your lot and other factors, but we're shooting for averages here.

Note that while you will get cut more in the summer and less during the winter, most services will charge you the same each month. It just helps them keep a steady cash flow and I think it helps the homeowner too so its pretty easy to remember what to pay.

Trimming of trees/shrubs is usually additional. I think if you budget $50-$75/month here you'd be pretty safe.

Pest Control

Most people especially those coming from up north never think of this one. You're going to want to have your yard sprayed for pests, as well as the inside of your home too. Some companies recommend monthly service, others say you can get by with quarterly. In either case, expect this to set you back $80-100/month.

Termite Bond

No matter what type of home you buy, do not go without a termite bond. Count on paying at least $100-$200/yr. for this.

Exterior Maintenance

You might want to budget for having the outside of your home pressure washed once or twice a year and painted every 5-7 years. Pressure washing will probably run $200-$300 per visit, and painting for an 1,800 sq. ft. home should be between $2,500 and $4,000.

Some Florida communities are what'd described as "maintenance-free" or have sections within them that are of this type, and this type of exterior maintenance will be done for you and the costs rolled into your monthly fees.

Groceries

Groceries are a tough one to estimate, so I would just use what you spend now as a starting point. There's quite a bit of choice in most areas here with Publix, Winn-Dixie, Walmart, Target, etc., so the competition helps keep prices in check.

Drinks and Eating Out

Same for restaurant and drink prices. There are lots of choices, and the competition keeps the prices in line. You don't have to look too hard to find coupons and deals enticing enough for just about any budget.

But, because of the number of choices, most of which are just a short golf cart ride away, residents find themselves eating out and/or socializing with new friends more than they ever have in the past.

So, to be safe, add 20-30% on to whatever your budget is now for drinking and eating out, not because prices are higher, but because you will likely be doing it more often.

Golf

Maybe you're a golfer or maybe not, but in The Villages, you get free golf for life on the executive courses if you walk. But, there is a small fee for golf cart rental. You can also use your own cart and pay a trail fee either daily, semi-annually, or annually.

You've got several options as it relates to Priority Championship Course Memberships, but on the high end they are currently $925 per couple (rates are less for singles) and this includes use of the Country Club pools, your executive trail fee and tennis at Hacienda Hills.

You also have to pay greens fees on top of this, though you do get a slight discount with this priority membership.

Again, to reiterate, this is information specific to one community. You'll need to research the rates at whatever communities you are considering.

Golf Cart

This will likely be one of the first purchases you make after buying your home, and many even complete this purchase before buying their home! Prices, styles and options for golf carts are almost as varied as for homes. You can find used carts in the classifieds or in some stores for less than $2000 or you can spend more than $20,000 for a tricked-out custom cart. The choice is yours but don't forget to budget for this expense.

You'll also need golf cart insurance. Like anything else it's good to shop around. Ask your cart dealer or salesman for a recommendation. I've seen rates range between $60/year to more than $200/year.

Roadside Service

Like cars, golf carts get flat tires, dead batteries, etc. A couple companies offer roadside assistance for yearly fees ranging from about $30/yr. to $60/yr. depending on the level of service you'd like.

Entertainment and Movies

You'll never be short on entertainment options in The Villages. You've got nightly entertainment in the town squares which is free. There are also ticketed shows, musical acts, Polo matches, etc. with ticket prices ranging from just a few bucks to more than $100+ depending on the act and the venue.

At one point The Villages operated a movie theater in each town square, but for various reasons they are now down to one. Ticket prices are currently $8.50 for residents showing a resident ID.

Newspapers

The Villages Daily Sun is currently about $88/year. I say "about" because the price varies slightly based on where your home is located. While you should probably subscribe just to keep up with daily events/happenings you're not going to see any hardcore news reporting. Because of this, many also get the Orlando Sentinel which is about $90 for 13 weeks if you want 7-day delivery. Less expensive options are available for Thursday and Sunday delivery, or Thursday through Sunday delivery.

Housewatch service

If you're going to be a seasonal resident, you'll probably want to look into a housewatch service, and these range from $35-$50/month depending on the level of service you want.

Various "One-Time" Costs

A lot of people fail to consider the many "one-time" costs they might incur when first moving to Florida. Prices vary greatly for things like adding gutters, screening in your lanai, buying new patio furniture, adding decorative curbing, interior painting, and more.

You can plan on at least $5,000 worth of this type of stuff needing to be done at a minimum. Just remember to take these into account when doing your budgeting/financial planning.

Again, my numbers are not necessarily your numbers, and your actual cost of living will depend on a number of factors, but hopefully this chapter gives you a good start and some food for thought.

CHAPTER SIXTEEN
PROPERTY TAXES

WHEN PEOPLE who are looking to buy in Florida ask me about the taxes, I like to share a little bit of humor. I say Florida has no state income tax, so they make up for it with real estate taxes and speeding tickets. Speeding tickets is the funny part. The real estate taxes, on the other hand, are not so funny for some.

The real estate taxes that you pay on a home can vary widely depending on what city and what county you are buying the home in. For example, taxes on a $350,000 home in one county could be around $6000, and taxes on the same priced home in another county could be around $4000.

Why the difference? Well, several factors are at work here, but one thing I've witnessed is that the taxes will usually be higher in areas that are experiencing rapid population and housing growth. When rapid growth happens some local governments cannot provide the level of services expected of them without raising taxes.

This usually happens because city governments didn't anticipate the rapid growth and must then play catch-up. Had they foreseen the growth, it might be a different story. They could have used the expanding tax base from more people moving into the area to increase the amount and level of services that would be needed such as building new roads and infrastructure, providing adequate schools, police, medical, and fire services, and hiring more public servants to oversee and run them.

Property Appraisal

The property appraiser's office has the task of putting a value on your home. This will help determine the amount of tax you will be required to pay. The property appraiser is not; however, the person who determines what your taxes will be. The local government does that when they set the millage rate.

Luckily, most of the time, you won't pay taxes on the entire price of your home. In Florida, property appraisers have a duty to assess your home at "just value." The typical property valuation is targeted between about 85-95 percent (but these are sometimes lower and sometimes higher) of what they think a particular property would sell for. If you just purchased a property, you are assessed at 85-95 percent of the amount you paid for it, that is, your contract price.

The property appraiser's job involves figuring out a reasonable range of values that buyers would pay for a particular property. Property assessments are usually set at the lower end of that range, which is normally around 85 percent. This is a practice used in almost all Florida counties. You will have to check with the property appraiser's office in the area you are considering to determine where in this range they prefer to target.

Many people wonder why the figures of 85-95 percent are used and not 100 percent. The lower figures are used to allow for closing costs, transfer taxes, and real estate commissions that may have been built into the final sales price but are not really part of the "value" in the home.

While the above information is good to know, in order to get the possible "worst-case scenario" idea of what your taxes will be, use the 100 percent value for your financial planning. Then when you get your tax bill, if it happens to be lower, you will hopefully be pleasantly surprised.

Millage Rate

An essential element to figuring out how much your taxes will be is the millage rate, commonly referred to as "mil rate." The millage rate is expresses as "mils per thousand." For example if the millage rate is "17", then you will pay $17 per $1,000 of assessed value.

Each taxing district will set its own millage rate which can be determined by dividing the total proposed budget of the taxing district (city, county, school district, etc.) by the total taxable value of all real estate in the district after exemptions are deducted for.

You will likely be taxed by your city, county, school district, water management district if there is one, and others. It's important to get a whole tax picture view before deciding on an area. The local property appraiser's office will usually be your best resource for this.

It is also important to note that real estate taxes in Florida are paid in arrears, and you will have an opportunity to get a small discount for paying them early.

For links to the property appraiser's offices throughout Florida visit:

floridarevenue.com/property/Pages/LocalOfficials.aspx

Once you find out the millage for the area you are buying a home in, you can use this formula to figure out an estimate of your taxes:

Price you pay for the home	$250,000
times	x
90% (assuming middle of 85–95% range)	90%
equals	=
"Just value"	$225,000
Divided by 1,000	/1000
equals	225
Times mil rate (we'll assume 17 mils per thousand)	x 17
Equals your tax liability	$3,825

State of Florida Homestead Exemptions

The state of Florida does provide some much-needed tax relief in the form of homestead exemptions.

$50,000 Homestead Exemption

Florida's constitution provides homeowners the right to receive a homestead exemption provided they meet certain residency requirements. Every person who has "legal or equitable title (you own it) to real property (your home) in the State of Florida and who resides on the property on January 1, and in good faith makes it his or her permanent home is eligible for a homestead exemption." This exemption reduces your "just value" by $50,000, which could save you around $1,000 on your property tax bill, depending on what the millage rate is for your area. For this example I assumed a 2% tax rate (20 mils).

HOWEVER, the second $25,000 of this $50,000 exemption does not apply to school taxes (which equate to about a third of most tax bills). Therefore, the actual benefit from this is closer to $15,000 (for a total benefit of $40,000....$25,000 + $15,000). The tax savings from a $40,000 exemption where this tax rate is 2% would be $800. Still not a bad chunk of change.

You have to make application with your county property appraiser's office for homestead exemption between January 1 of the previous year and March 1 of the year you want the exemption. For example, for the 2022 tax year, you would have been able to apply for homestead exemption from January 1, 2021 to March 1, 2022.

When filing your homestead exemption for the first time, you will be asked to provide evidence that you are a legal resident, such as a voter registration card or a Florida driver's license. Most counties have automatic renewal programs so there is no need to reapply each year as long as you are in the same home. If you move, however, you will need to reapply.

If you are a part-time resident using your home in Florida as a vacation home or second home, you will not be eligible for this exemption.

Other Possible Exemptions

In addition to the $50,000 Homestead Exemption, there are other exemptions available that could possibly reduce your tax bill.

Additional Homestead Exemption for Persons 65 and Older of up to $25,000

This exemption is available on a county-by-county basis, and not all counties offer it.

$500 Widow's and Widower's Exemption

This one is pretty self-explanatory.

$500 Disability Exemption

Any Florida resident who is totally and permanently disabled may claim this exemption with proper documentation of the disability.

$5,000 Disability Exemption for Ex -Service Members

An ex-service member who is disabled at least 10 percent in war or another service-related incident might be entitled to this exemption.

Exemption for Deployed Military

A member or former member of any branch of the United States military or military reserves, the United States Coast Guard or its reserves, or the Florida National Guard may receive an exemption on this year's tax bill if he or she receives a homestead exemption, was deployed during the last calendar year outside the continental United States, Alaska, and Hawaii in support of a designated operation (each year the Florida legislature designates operations for this exemption), and submits an application, Form DR-501M, to the property appraiser.

The percent of the taxable value that is exempt for the current year is determined by the percent of time during the last year when the service member was deployed on a designated operation.

$500 Exemption for Blind Persons

In order to claim this exemption, you must have a certificate of blindness issued by the Division of Blind Services of the Department of Education, the Federal Social Security Administration, or the Veteran's Administration.

These exemptions can be combined with each other. Certain other rules and restrictions apply to the above exemptions. You should contact the local property appraiser's office for more information on the county in which you are interested.

Save Our Homes

The Save Our Homes amendment is a piece of legislation which helps limit the tax burden of those residents who own homesteaded property in Florida.

Over the period of 2001-2005 home prices rose by as much as 100 percent or more in many parts of Florida. Most people would have a hard time handling a property tax bill increase of 100 percent in such a short period of time. In fact, in such situations, many homeowners of modest means on fixed incomes would no longer be able to afford the home they live in because they wouldn't be able to pay the taxes.

The Save Our Homes amendment states that the change in assessed value of a homesteaded property cannot exceed 3 percent of the assessed value of the property for the prior year or the percentage change of the Consumer Price Index as reported by the U.S. Department of Labor, Bureau of Labor Statistics, whichever is lower.

Using an example from several years ago, the Consumer Price Index rose 3.8 percent in 2008, so the increase in assessed value was capped at 3.00 percent. For illustrative purposes let's assume that between 2007 and 2008 the value of your home in Florida doubled from $100,000 to $200,000. With the Save Our Homes cap, you could only be taxed on

$103,000 ($100K + 3 percent) instead of the full value of $200,000.

Already live in Florida and plan on moving elsewhere within the state for retirement? It's a little tricky, but in many circumstances up to $500,000 of any Save Our Homes benefit you may have accrued can go with you to your next house. If you are moving from out of state this doesn't affect you. Only if you live in Florida, are homesteaded, and have built up Save Our Homes benefits does it apply, but you'll want to check with the property appraiser's office in both the county you currently live in and the county you are moving to (if they are different) to ensure you do everything you need to qualify for this benefit.

Property Tax Disclosure

Once a home changes ownership, it is reassessed at its full value, and the Save Our Homes amendment does not go back into effect until a year after the property is homesteaded again. This is assuming the new owner is not bringing built up Save Our Homes tax savings with them like I mentioned in the last paragraph (i.e.: they are moving from out of state, etc.).

Consider this scenario. You are looking at a house on the market for $400,000. The Multiple Listing Service printout that your agent gives you on the property states that the amount of property taxes paid by the owner for the prior year was $2,500. It is a very common but costly mistake for buyers to assume their property taxes will be that same amount.

I've heard "but it says right there on the sheet, Property Tax: $2,500" too many times. The truth is that your taxes could be much higher because you will be required to pay taxes on the amount that you pay for the property. The current owner is paying taxes based on what they paid for the property, which, depending on when they bought the property, could be considerably less.

The Florida Legislature thought that not enough people buying homes were being made aware of this fact so they introduced a new Property Tax Disclosure which must be in all residential real estate contracts. It reads:

BUYER SHOULD NOT RELY ON THE SELLER'S CURRENT PROPERTY TAXES AS THE AMOUNT OF PROPERTY TAXES THAT THE BUYER MAY BE OBLIGATED TO PAY IN THE YEAR SUBSEQUENT TO PURCHASE. A CHANGE OF OWNERSHIP OR PROPERTY IMPROVEMENTS TRIGGERS REASSESSMENTS OF THE PROPERTY THAT COULD RESULT IN HIGHER PROPERTY TAXES. IF YOU HAVE ANY QUESTIONS CONCERNING VALUATION, CONTACT THE COUNTY PROPERTY APPRAISER'S OFFICE FOR INFORMATION.

As the last sentence of that disclosure states, the best resource for calculating what your taxes will be on a particular property is the local Property Appraiser's office. They are there to help you.

CHAPTER SEVENTEEN
RENTALS

SEVERAL TIMES A WEEK I get questions about finding rentals in Florida retirement communities, so I hope some of you will find this chapter helpful.

First Off, Why Rent?

The first question some of you might be asking, is why would somebody want to rent? Isn't that just pouring money down the drain to help pay off someone else's mortgage?

A while back the real estate website Trulia.com did a study and determined that yes, it is in fact cheaper to buy than it is to rent for retirement, at least in Florida. On the other hand others will argue, you have to live somewhere, and whether you buy or rent, it's going to cost money.

Financial aspects aside, there are other reasons why some people will decide to opt for a Florida retirement community rental. Here are a few I can think of off the top of my head that I've heard over the years.

Not Sure Where You Want to Settle Down

This is probably the most common reason I hear for retirees wanting to rent, and I don't think it's a terrible idea to rent for a little while if you don't have a solid grasp on where you want to settle down. Renting for a while will give you a chance to get to know an area before you make a firm commitment.

Flexibility

Somewhat related to the first reason someone might want to rent is flexibility. A lot of people like more than one area, and they want to be able to easily move to a new location every few years.

Only Want to Live in Florida Part-Time

And of course, you have those who will only call Florida home part of the year, and don't want to pay for a home here year-round so they find a part-time rental, whether that is a 3-month winter rental or perhaps they do a 6 months here, 6 months there type of thing.

Location, Location, Location

A lot of people approach this process focused on the actual houses for rent first, and to me that's backwards. Just like the methodology I describe in my book Pick the Right Place, you should think of going about finding a rental in terms of location, then community, then home.

Once you have one or a tiny handful of locations picked out, you can start to look around online and see what kinds of rentals might be available.

Where to Look

Of course there are hundreds, maybe even thousands of websites advertising rentals, but you can save yourself some time at this point in your search by focusing on some of the bigger websites.

For long-term rentals, your best bets will be sites like Zillow.com and Realtor.com. Make sure you've selected "For Rent", enter the area you are interested in, selected any other criteria you want, and see what you can find.

For short-term rentals, websites like VRBO.com and Home-Away.com might be your best bet.

If you exhaust each of those sites, you can throw a "Hail Mary" and do a Google search like "Location" + "Rentals" or "Location" + "Property Management" (note that the "+" is not required), but these days most management companies syndicate their listings to the bigger sites I mentioned.

Community: For Rentals, Size Matters

Once you've selected a location and explored what might be available, you should next zero in on a few communities that might fit your needs.

For people looking to buy in a Florida retirement community, I suggest they focus on communities of all sizes...big, small, and in-between that suit their needs. But for those looking for

Florida retirement community rentals, I often suggest they focus on the larger communities for a couple reasons.

The first should be obvious; the more homes a community has, generally the more rentals there will be available for you to choose from. Along with that, it can also sometimes be nice to not be the only, or one of just a few, renters in a community.

Some homeowners can be weird, and they might not include you as quickly or build a relationship with you as fast knowing that you are a renter that could up and leave at the end of your lease. That's not always the case of course, but I've seen it happen and it's something to think about.

Before we leave the topic of communities, a lot of people reach out asking me if any of the new communities that I mention on my site offer rentals. While there may be rentals in newer communities, understand that most developers are in the business of building and selling homes, not renting them.

In fact, most make no mention of rentals anywhere on their websites and do not engage in the practice, so unfortunately with rentals, you're going to have to do a lot of the legwork on your own.

Could you strike up a conversation with a new home salesperson who just happens to know of a homeowner looking for a renter? It's possible, but again, their focus is going to be more on selling homes, not on helping you find a rental.

Property Manager vs. Owner Manager

As you progress in your rental search you'll see some homes that are managed by the homeowner, and others that are managed by real estate companies.

My suggestion is to focus as much as possible on the homes that are managed by real estate companies. That way you've got a licensed 3rd party involved, striving to keep you and the owner of the property happy.

Could you luck out with an owner-managed rental? Of course, it happens all the time, but I've been at this a long time and if you were related to me I would try to advise you against going the managed by-owner route.

Most rental management companies have policies and procedures in place to handle any number of issues that can arise, but with an individual owner, you just never know. This is just one example, but what if your A/C goes out in the middle of July, but the owner is on vacation out of the country and you can't reach them?

Now, hopefully your rental agreement speaks to what happens in cases like this, but I'd just sleep better at night knowing there's an actual company I can get ahold of when I need. I think you get the idea, but of course you are the best judge of what's best for you.

I hope this chapter has given you some things to think about, and if you do decide to rent here in Florida, I hope it helps you find a great rental. Good luck!

IF SPENDING the cold winter months living in sunny Florida is something that you have often thought about but never really explored, today is the day for you to start thinking a bit more seriously about wintering in Florida.

With a history that dates back to brilliant minds like John D. Rockefeller, Henry Ford, and Thomas Edison, the snowbird concept of heading south to Florida for the winter has long been popular among just about anyone that can afford it.

And with the ease of travel, the power of the internet, and plenty of reasonably priced real estate, the snowbird dream has never been more attainable than it is today.

When is Snowbird Season?

As a general rule, snowbird season here in Florida kicks off at the beginning of October and our seasonal residents will continue to trickle in all the way through the end of the holiday season.

Depending on where the snowbirds are coming from, they tend to head back home for the summer sometime during the months of April and May.

How Many Snowbirds Come to Florida?

It is nearly impossible to get a true number that distinguishes snowbirds from regular tourists, but by most estimates the number of snowbirds coming to Florida each year is typically in the very high six figures.

That means that the population of Florida actually grows by as much as 5% during the snowbird-friendly winter months.

One of the less scientific ways to measure the impact of snowbirds on the population of an individual community is to simply take note of the differences in terms of traffic on the streets and crowds at popular restaurants.

The effect is even more pronounced in popular retirement communities like The Villages where, even with nearly 700 holes of golf, it can be a challenge to get a tee time on some of the more popular courses during the winter months.

How Long Can Snowbirds Stay?

While American snowbirds don't have to worry about any limitations on the amount of time that they are permitted to stay in Florida, things are a bit more complicated for snowbirds coming from countries like Canada.

The long-standing rule for Canadian snowbirds is that they are allowed to stay in Florida for up to six months at a time on what is known as a B1/B2 visa. However, there is currently proposed legislation with bipartisan support to get Congress to push this limit to eight months.

Should Snowbirds Get Local IDs?

One of the most common questions we see from future Florida snowbirds is whether or not they will need to update their state identification or driver's licenses. The answer to these questions depend on a few different factors.

The main thing to consider is what state you are going to claim as your primary residence. The majority of snowbirds prefer to remain residents of their original states, and thus maintain their identification according to the laws of that state.

However, since there are tax advantages that come with living in Florida (more on that in a bit), there are some snowbirds who prefer to claim Florida as their primary residence instead.

There are a number of legal concerns when it comes to claiming residence on your personal tax returns, so you will definitely want to consult with your accountant on this issue.

Once you have a good understanding of which state you are going to call home on your tax returns, then you can worry about maintaining proper identification according to that state's specifications.

How Does Healthcare Work for Snowbirds?

Another common question from aspiring snowbirds is how their healthcare will work when they begin spending as much as half of the year in a different state.

In most cases, whatever type of health insurance that a snowbird has will be accepted just about anywhere in the country, which means that it will work fine here in Florida.

Of course, you will still have to find a new network of doctors that you feel comfortable with near your winter home, but there are plenty of excellent resources for doing just that here in Florida.

The only real issues to be cautious of concerning healthcare are people who have policies with very specific coverage areas. If your health insurance is only good for a small network near your original home, you won't be able to use it here in Florida.

Another group of snowbirds that will always have health insurance challenges are Canadians that spend the winters in Florida.

Anyone who is not able to bring their health coverage with them to Florida will likely want to purchase some type of private coverage to ensure they can get the proper treatment they need during the winter months.

Finding Winter Rentals for Snowbirds

While there is certainly a large portion of snowbirds that own their own winter properties here in Florida, there are just as many snowbirds that prefer rentals instead.

Renting a Florida home for a few months during the winter is a fantastic way to get started living the snowbird dream, and finding those winter rentals is easier today than it has ever been.

Airbnb and VRBO are also good places to start any search for these kinds of rentals, and you can find properties for all locations and budgets here in Florida on either site.

In addition to those mainstream sites, there are also plenty of local management companies operating rentals all over Florida. You can find most of them by simply typing something like "CITY NAME property management" or "CITY NAME winter Rentals" into your favorite search box.

While sites like Airbnb and VRBO will give you the most options, finding a local property management company will give you other advantages like more personalized service and faster responses to any issues that might arise during your stay.

Buying a Winter Home in Florida

Renting a winter home in Florida is a perfect way to get started enjoying the snowbird experience, but most snowbirds have the long-term goal of purchasing their own winter home eventually.

Once you are fairly certain about the snowbird lifestyle and find the perfect location, owning a winter home in Florida offers a host of financial benefits that make it a better deal for most snowbirds in the long run.

But there are also plenty of issues that come with owning a second residence in another state.

Maintaining Multiple Homes

One of the best things about owning multiple homes in this modern age is that we have a plethora of technology available to make the process a whole lot easier than it was even just a few years ago.

With services like Nest and Ring, you can monitor live cameras set up around any of your homes at any time you like. These services can be as simple as a single camera looking at the front door, or they can include a more complicated multi-camera setup that lets you see every room in the house.

These modern technologies give you the ability to check in on your home from anywhere in the world.

Finding Someone to Keep an Eye on the Place

All of the technology in the world will never give us the peace of mind that comes from having a real human check in on our homes when we are not there, and no one knows this better than snowbirds.

Because of this, there are plenty of companies that will be happy to make sure everything is running smoothly at either of your homes when you aren't around.

All it takes is a quick search for something along the lines of "snowbird home watch" and you will be well on your way to finding a reputable company to keep an eye on your place for you.

Of course, there is an even easier method that has been working for years: good neighbors!

If you are blessed to have wonderful neighbors that you trust in either location, that is always going to be your best bet for having someone you trust to keep an eye on your home for you.

Renting Your Winter Home Out During the Summer

Snowbirds who purchase a winter home here in Florida also have the option to rent out that home during the months that they aren't planning to use it.

In addition to providing a source of income that can offset some of the cost of the property, this is also a great way to make sure that someone is keeping up with basic maintenance and keeping the place in good shape while you aren't there.

The easiest way to rent out your Florida home during any time of the year is to partner with a local management company. However, you can also manage rentals on your own through sites like Airbnb.com or VRBO.com.

Using the power of the internet to manage your own rentals will definitely save you a few bucks, but working with a local management company will provide a truly hands-off experience. So you have to weigh the pros and cons of each option and decide which one is right for you.

Choosing Your State of Residence

After buying a winter home in Florida, many snowbirds begin to consider whether it would make sense for them to change their permanent residence to Florida and travel back to their summer home as a visitor.

Again, there are a number of tax advantages that come with living in Florida, but there are also plenty of rules that come with making that change, so you will definitely want to discuss this with your accountant before filing any paperwork.

Changing your permanent residence will also impact your driver's license, voting location, and many other factors of life that you are accustomed to. Plus it will require you to spend a certain minimum number of nights here in Florida, which may be more than you originally planned for.

Final Thoughts on Snowbirding

Regardless of whether you are a first-time snowbird looking to visit for a month or a regular snowbird looking to expand your commitment to the Sunshine State, there are many paths to happiness for snowbirds of all types here in Florida.

The best way to get the most out of your snowbird experience is to write down exactly what you want it to be and then find a way to make that lifestyle happen.

IN ADDITION to the obvious need to protect your investment, the ability to get homeowner's insurance is of utmost importance when getting a mortgage on your property. No mortgage company will loan you money without you first having insurance on the property. In some instances your mortgage lender can even foreclose on the property if you fail to carry insurance. While no one can predict what the future will bring, I have done my best to compile for you the facts and resources, as they now stand, to help you navigate the homeowner's insurance minefield in Florida.

Current State of the Florida Property Insurance Market

Even before Hurricanes Ian and Nicole blew through Florida in 2022, the Florida Property Insurance Market had been in turmoil. Some Florida homeowners are experiencing 20-40% property insurance rate increases, and some with older homes, particularly with roofs that are more than a decade old, have been dropped by their insurance carriers altogether.

While it's too early to tell the extent of the effects Hurricanes Ian and Nicole will have on the property insurance market, it's important to note that inclement weather events like hurricanes have not been the source of Florida's property insurance troubles.

So what is the main culprit? According to most experts it's litigation, much of which is due to scams and unwarranted claims. According to multiple reports I've read, as much as 75% of all homeowners insurance litigation in the country in recent years has been in Florida.

One popular scam has attorneys and roofing contractors part-nering up to convince homeowners to file unwarranted damage claims with their insurance companies. The contractors canvas neighborhoods, typically those with older and more upscale homes (think: bigger roofs), going door to door telling homeowners that they have roof damage and they can get it fixed or replaced for free by assigning their insurance benefits over to the contractor.

In this scam the contractor would often replace the roof, which could have simply had one loose shingle (or no damage at all) and file a claim with the homeowner's insurance company without submitting any evidence of the damage. Keep in mind normal wear and tear on a roof is not covered by insurance, so only events like hail damage or windstorm damage would typically qualify as a "claimable incident".

When or if the insurance company denies the claim, the attorneys involved in the scheme file a lawsuit against the insurance company. They of course go after the amount of the unpaid claim, but also for their attorney fees which often amount to more than what the initial claim amount was for.

Until just recently, if the court found in favor of the plaintiff (homeowner/roofer/attorney) in any amount, even for just $1, the attorney would be awarded their full fees. In addition, Florida had a one-way attorney fee statute in place which meant that even if the court found for the defendant (insurer) they could not recoup their own legal costs for fighting the claim.

This one-way fee statute was intended to protect policy-holders against legal recourse if they wanted to sue their insurers for denied or lowballed claims, but you can see in this example how laws made with good intentions can go awry. You can also see why for the attorneys willing to take up this scheme it's a "heads I win, tails you lose" kind of situation.

With laws like these stacked against them, some insurance companies have found it cheaper to just pay the claims rather than fight the scam, but this of course has driven up insurance rates for the rest of their customers, and has led to some insurers refusing to offer coverage in certain areas, and in some cases packing up shop and leaving the state completely.

The good news is that these issues are on the radar of our state's elected leaders, and reforms put in place as recently as this year have eliminated some of the ridiculous advantages available to those running scams like this one. But, some experts think it will take time to see if the recent legal changes will be enough to stabilize the Florida property insurance market.

Finding Coverage

With all of that in mind, how should you go about finding property insurance here in Florida?

Presumably you now have homeowner's insurance on your current residence, wherever that might be. My first piece of advice is to ask your current insurance agent if their company writes homeowner's insurance policies in Florida. If you are with a large national insurer with operations in Florida, the odds are good that they do write homeowner's policies in Florida.

By doing this, you are taking the path of least resistance, and you will probably be able to get pretty decent rates through what are called "multi-line" discounts assuming you have other property such as cars, jewelry and the like already insured through them. You are welcome to shop around and price out other insurers, but from what I've seen, if you are comfortable with the company you have now, switching carriers to save a few bucks isn't worth the hassle.

Ask Around

If that does not work out, my next step would be to ask any family or friends currently living in Florida who they have as their homeowner's insurance carrier. If they have no useful information, ask your real estate agent, mortgage broker, new home salesperson, or potential new neighbors for recommendations.

You may have to do some legwork, phoning different agencies to see who is offering what kinds of coverage at the time you need insurance. Some companies also have a one policy out, one policy in type of arrangement, where they will place you on a waiting list and when a policyholder does not renew for whatever reason, they can pick you up.

Florida Market Assistance Program

If you've tried all of the above and still are not able to get coverage, your next step is to visit the website of the Florida Market Assistance Program at fmap.org. FMAP is a free online referral service, created by the Florida legislature and designed to connect those who are not able to find coverage with insurers who are able to write new policies. You register at the website and submit a request for quotes. Agents will typically then call or e-mail you if they can offer assistance to you based on where your home is located, its age, and other factors.

For more information visit:

fmap.org/consumers

The Last Resort

If all of the above options fail and you are not able to find private homeowner's insurance coverage, Citizens Property Insurance Corporation is your last available option.

The Florida Legislature created Citizen's in 2002 to help Floridians who cannot get traditional coverage. More than half a million homeowners in Florida now turn to Citizens for their homeowner's insurance coverage. All those customers dropped by their insurance companies? Most of them are now Citizen's customers.

Between October 2020 and October 2021, Citizen's policy count grew from 521,289 to 725,942. By October 2022 that figure was 1,098,762.

You should first try to get your coverage elsewhere, but at least you know that Citizen's is an option if nobody else will write you a policy.

For more information visit:

citizensfla.com

Cash Value vs. Replacement Cost

When shopping for homeowner's insurance, there are various types of coverage available for you to choose from, including "actual cash value" and "replacement cost coverage". I've always been told, and I believe it to be true, that guaranteed replacement cost coverage is the type of coverage you should be after.

With an actual cash value policy, if you are insured for $200,000 and repairs to your damaged home cost $250,000 the insurance company will be covering $200,000. Guaranteed replacement cost coverage means that even if you are insured for $200,000, if your home is destroyed and it costs

$250,000 to build at today's construction costs to be put back into use as it was before, then that's what the insurance company will pay.

Replacement cost coverage will cost more, as you might imagine, but it provides the policyholder with much more protection. One way to mitigate the rise in your premium is to raise your deductible. When you raise your deductible, or the amount you pay out of pocket to file a claim, your yearly premiums will go down.

Windstorm and Hail Insurance

The insurance company that I've always used (State Farm) includes windstorm and hail insurance in their basic homeowner's policy. I'm not sure if that's how every insurance company operates, but I know that most mortgage companies require this coverage. The rates vary based on where your property is located, what kind of roof you have, whether or not you have hurricane shutters or impact resistant windows, and so on.

But not all types of insurance you might want or need to consider here in Florida are automatically included, which brings us to flood and sinkhole insurance.

Flood Insurance

There are two facts that most people do not know. First, flooding is the number one natural disaster in the United States; even properties not near water can be susceptible to flooding. Second, losses due to floods are not covered by your homeowner's insurance policy.

The Federal Emergency Management Agency (FEMA) puts out "flood maps" that show which areas tend to be most prone to flooding. I often hear people ask, "is the property in a flood zone?" and usually people describing homes in low-risk areas will say "no, it's not in a flood zone." Well, the correct answer is that every property is in a flood zone. It's just a matter of whether it is in a low, moderate, or high-risk flood zone.

Your real estate agent might be able to tell you which flood zone the property you are looking at is in, and there are a few online resources available to help you determine this (links at the end of this chapter). But it is your insurance agent who will use a Flood Insurance Rate Map or FIRM, to ultimately determine your flood risk. Be aware that federal law requires you to purchase flood insurance if you have a federally backed mortgage and reside in a high-risk area.

In my opinion, everyone, no matter where in Florida they live should carry flood insurance which is available through the National Flood Insurance Program (NFIP).

In most cases, the insurance company that handles your regular homeowner's insurance coverage will be able to help you secure this.

In an effort to keep the NFIP solvent, FEMA rolled out changes in October 2021 that, in their words, "fundamentally change the way FEMA prices insurance and determines an individual property's flood risk" and "delivers rates that more accurately reflect flood risk and ensure the National Flood

Insurance Program will be here for this generation and generations to come".

The new changes go beyond considering simply whether a property is in a low, moderate, or high-risk flood zone, and takes into account other variables like potential flood frequency, flood type, a property's distance to a water source, elevation, cost to rebuild, and more.

When I researched flood insurance rates before these changes, you could get $250,000 of building and $100,000 of contents coverage for about $420/year in a low-risk flood zone.

According to FEMA, with these new changes about 20% of covered Floridians will see a rate decrease (though they don't specify how much of a decrease), 68% will see a $0-$120/year increase, 8% will see a $120-$240/year increase, and 4% will see a greater than $240/year increase.

It pains me to type this, but unfortunately I know someone personally who fell into the category of the 68% that saw a rate increase, decided to let their flood insurance policy expire, and then got flooded by Hurricane Ian. Their house was in a low-risk flood zone and their increase was only going to be about $50/year. Now they are spending tens of thousands to repair and replace things this policy would have covered.

Please don't make the same mistake. Get the flood insurance!

For more information on flood zones, flood maps, and flood insurance contact your insurance agent or visit these websites:

floodsmart.gov

riskfactor.com

Sinkhole Insurance

Florida has more sinkholes than any other state. This is because in many parts of Florida, the ground near the surface is sitting on top of limestone. When underground water levels rise and fall, this limestone can dissolve and form holes. When the ground below is no longer strong enough to support the weight of what is on top, there may be a sinkhole. Sinkholes can happen anywhere, but if you research this topic on your own, most websites will tell you that North Central and West Central Florida are where they seem to occur most often.

For insurance purposes, it's important to distinguish between what's known as Catastrophic Ground Cover Collapse coverage, and sinkhole coverage. They are two different things.

Florida law requires all homeowner's insurance policies to include Catastrophic Ground Cover Collapse (CGCC) coverage, but there is strict criteria that must be met for an incident to be covered:

1. The abrupt collapse of the ground cover;

2. depression in the ground cover clearly visible to the naked eye;

3. Structural damage to the building including the foundation; and

4. The insured structure being condemned and ordered to be vacated by the government agency authorized by law to issue such an order for that structure."

If a sinkhole occurs and any one of those four criteria is not met, the incident will likely not be covered by your insurance company. If you read those criteria again, you'll note that your home must literally be condemned and vacated for CGCC coverage to kick in. There have been efforts in the state legislature to change this but as of this writing nothing has made it out of the proposal stage.

Fortunately (in the case of safety) or unfortunately (in the case of your ability to collect insurance money to fix your home), most sinkholes do not cause enough damage to meet this criteria.

That's where optional sinkhole coverage comes in. Florida law requires all insurance companies writing policies in Florida to *offer* sinkhole coverage, typically as a separate policy or in a rider, and of course this will be at an additional charge above and beyond what your regular insurance costs. It's also important to note that if geological testing or an inspection reveals that sinkhole activity is present on your property or within a certain distance of it, the insurance company can decline to provide sinkhole coverage to you.

While actual geological testing can cost thousands of dollars, most insurance companies will simply send a representative out to do a walk around of the property and sometimes they'll come inside and inspect around windows and doors for signs of excessive settling before approving you for coverage.

To learn more about sinkholes and the availability of coverage in the areas you are looking contact an insurance agent or visit:

floridadep.gov/FGS/Sinkholes

CHAPTER TWENTY
HURRICANES 101

I KNOW you might think I'm crazy to say this right after Hurricanes Ian and Nicole crossed Florida from different sides a little over a month apart in 2022, but if you're thinking about Florida for retirement, I hope you won't let the thought of hurricanes keep you away.

Since Hurricane Andrew destroyed the city of Homestead in South Florida near Miami in 1992, Florida has enacted some of the toughest building codes in the country, and they get more stringent every couple of years.

To be sure, the damage you typically see on the news is most often at older properties, built well before the 1990's and 2000's when these new building code changes were made.

Where you build, of course, also has an impact. Coastal areas will typically experience more damage than inland areas, usually due to flooding. Homes on lots with few trees will experience less damage than homes on heavily wooded lots. Common sense type stuff.

Building codes aren't the only thing that have improved since Hurricane Andrew in the 1990's. Government response both before and after storms has also vastly improved.

Hurricane Season

The season officially begins June 1 and runs through November 30, with most activity typically occurring in late August through September. Most everyone who has lived in Florida for longer than a few years has been through at least one hurricane and several tropical storms. Though they are nothing to dismiss or joke about, with proper planning and precautions you'll be able to weather the storms like a native.

Tropical depressions, tropical storms and hurricanes, when present, dominate the news here in Florida. The attention is for good reason. Hurricanes produce extreme winds, tornadoes, torrential rain, and storm surge, which can cause severe flooding of coastal areas. In fact, nearly 60 percent of hurricane fatalities occur as a result of flooding. Other effects are of course property damage, power outages, temporary loss of public services, bridge and road closures, loss of communications, and hospital closures.

A hurricane usually begins as a tropical wave that develops into a low-pressure system known as a tropical depression. Tropical depressions are not very organized but they have the potential to become stronger and evolve into more organized storms. You can, and if you move to Florida most likely you will, track storm developments on-line at sites like weatherunderground.com or nhc.noaa.gov.

Tropical depressions have sustained winds of up to 38 mph. Should the storm gain strength, the next level is called a tropical storm, with winds between 39 and 73 mph, strong enough to cause pretty severe damage to older, unprotected structures.

Hurricane Watch versus Hurricane Warning

A Hurricane Watch indicates the possibility that you could experience hurricane conditions within 36 hours. This watch should trigger your family's disaster plan, and protective measures should be initiated.

A Hurricane Warning indicates that sustained winds of at least 74 mph are expected within 24 hours or less. Once this warning has been issued, your family should be in the process of completing protective actions and deciding the safest location to be during the storm.

Hurricane Ratings

Hurricanes are rated on a scale of 1-5 on the Saffir-Simpson Scale:

- Category One Hurricane: Winds 74-95 mph
- Category Two Hurricane: Winds 96-110 mph
- Category Three Hurricane: Winds 111-130 mph
- Category Four Hurricane: Winds 131-155
- Category Five Hurricane: Winds greater than 155 mph

The category ratings are based on the strength of the hurricane, not an expected level of its potential for destruction. Hypothetically, a category one hurricane hitting a highly populated area could cause more destruction than a category five hitting a less populated place. To read more about hurricane categories and the Saffir-Simpson scale visit:

nhc.noaa.gov/aboutsshws.php

Preparing for a Hurricane

If you do become a property owner in Florida, you should take great care in preparing your property and your household for the threat of hurricanes. Don't assume that because you live in the center of the state that you are immune from storm fallout.

Be prepared. Have a written hurricane plan. At the beginning of hurricane season, check your disaster kit, batteries and non-perishable food supply. Tips for developing a plan and building a hurricane kit can be found on-line at redcross.org and fema.gov. Local television news stations usually put out hurricane tracking guides, which have tips on what you should do to prepare.

According to FEMA, you should have these items on hand:

- Water: one gallon per person, per day (2-week supply)
- Food: non-perishable, easy-to-prepare items (2-week supply)
- Flashlight

- Battery-powered or hand-crank radio (NOAA Weather Radio)
- Extra batteries
- First aid kit
- Medications (7-day supply) and medical items
- Multi-purpose tool, like a Swiss Army knife
- Sanitation and personal hygiene items
- Copies of personal documents (medication list and pertinent medical information, proof of address, deed/lease to home, passports, birth certificates, insurance policies)
- Cell phone with charger
- Family and emergency contact information
- Extra cash (ATMs might be inoperable)
- Extra fuel for generator and car

Depending on your family's requirements, you may need to include medical-care items, baby supplies, pet supplies and other things, such as extra car and house keys. Additional supplies might include towels, plastic sheeting, duct tape, scissors and work gloves.

Also, no matter how secure you may feel in your home, if you are asked by local authorities to evacuate, you should do so and do so early. Prepare for traffic congestion and long lines at the gas pumps. It helps to have a plan in place regarding where you will go and what you will take with you. Yes, it is a pain and inconvenience to pack up your essentials, secure your home, and drive to safe territory, but it could also save your life.

CHAPTER TWENTY-ONE
REAL ESTATE CONTRACTS AND DISCLOSURES

ON THE NEXT page I've included a link to a standard "As Is" Florida real estate contract used by Realtors for most transactions. It's important to note that if you are buying a new home, most home builders have their own contracts.

Your real estate agent should be able to explain all of the important details of the standard Florida real estate contract. But if you are unsatisfied with their explanation you should not hesitate to contact a Florida real estate attorney.

A Note About Buying a Home "As-Is"

These days, in most markets, the majority of resale homes are marketed "as-is". The seller is still required to disclose all known facts that affect the value of the property. However, the seller makes no representation as to the physical condition of the property.

As the buyer in this scenario, you are given the right to inspect the property, and you are also given the right to cancel the contract, should you not be satisfied with the findings of the inspection or do not wish to pay for the repairs that need to be made.

You will be given a certain number of days to conduct your inspections and you must let the seller know of your intention to cancel in writing during that allotted time, should you decide you do not want to proceed with the purchase.

If your inspection turns up thousands of dollars in repairs that need to be done, you could negotiate with the seller to have them pay for some or all of the repairs. The outcome will depend on how willing you/they are to pay for the repairs, and how badly you want the house and/or how badly they want to sell.

Having a good inspection performed and working with a knowledgeable and skilled agent are key here.

Here's what the most recent version of the Standard "As Is" contract looks like:

s3.amazonaws.com/floridaforboomers/florida-asis-contract.pdf

Homeowners' Association Disclosure

The Homeowners' Association Disclosure, required by Florida Statute 720.401 is one of the more plainly written documents you will come across during your real estate transactions here in Florida. You can see an example here:

s3.amazonaws.com/floridaforboomers/Florida-HOA-Disclosure.pdf

Also note the statement in **BOLD CAPS** towards the top of the disclosure form. This simply means that if you completed a contract before receiving this notice, you may be able to void your contract if you so desire, within three days after having finally received this disclosure, or prior to closing, whichever comes first.

Florida Building Energy Efficiency Rating Disclosure

As the purchaser of a home in Florida you have the right to have the energy efficiency of the home tested. This can be helpful in determining what the annual energy use of the home might be, and how it compares to other homes used as "yardsticks" for means of comparison. You should be notified of this right either before doing a contract or at the time of contract. Most contracts will have verbiage in them alerting you to this fact.

For more information, check out a brochure on this at:

s3.amazonaws.com/floridaforboomers/florida-energy-brochure.pdf

New Home Sales Contracts and Disclosures

As I mentioned, if you plan on buying or building a new home, most homebuilders will use their own contracts and, right or wrong, they usually err on the side of protecting the builder more than you the customer.

With that in mind, here are a few things unique to new home builder contracts that you might encounter.

Right to Extend Closing Date

Your contract might specify an "estimated" completion date for your new home, but there's usually something in the contract that protects the builder in the case of unforeseen delays in completing your home. Unfortunately for buyers, this usually only works one way. If the builder is late delivering your home, you're typically on the hook for covering any expenses you might incur because of this delay. However, if you are the cause of any closing delays, they'll usually charge you a per day penalty for missing their closing date. My advice here is to try to remain as flexible as possible with your schedule and plans until you have a firm closing date.

No Buyer Alterations or Additions

In most cases, you will not be allowed to have any work performed by outside vendors while your new home is under construction. One example is let's say you don't care for the builder's available selection of ceiling fans. With this type of clause in your contract, you won't be able to have ceiling fans that you found somewhere else installed in your new home until after you close.

Age Verification Addendum

If you are buying a home in an age-restricted community, your contract will typically have a clause or addendum certifying that you in fact do meet the age requirements, and you'll usually be asked to provide some form of documentation to verify this like your driver's license, birth certificate, or passport.

Anti-Flipping Clause

Some communities have a clause in their new home sales contract that basically says that if you sell your home before a certain amount of time, usually before the 1-year mark, the developer gets any profit you make above what you paid for the home. This isn't a sneaky way for developers to make more money, but as the name suggests to prevent the practice of flipping, which is common whenever Florida experiences one of its real estate market booms.

Insulation Disclosure for New Construction Homes

If you are buying a new construction home in Florida, you must be given an Insulation Disclosure, either in the contract or as a separate rider attached to the contract. The type, thickness, and R-value of the insulation in the interior walls, exterior walls, and the ceilings in all areas should be disclosed to you.

CHAPTER TWENTY-TWO
HOME INSPECTIONS AND WARRANTIES

HOME INSPECTIONS and home warranties are two tools available to you that will help to ensure that the present and future condition of your new home here in Florida is satisfactory.

Home Inspections

Before finalizing the purchase of a home, you should always have a home inspection done. This point cannot be stressed enough. A home inspection could be the best money you ever spend. Home inspectors conduct a thorough evaluation of the home that can help you understand the condition that the house is actually in before you take ownership. Remember, that sometimes looks can be deceiving, and nobody likes unexpected surprises or costly repairs once they move in. Even if the house is fairly new and appears to be in good condition, you never know what could be hiding out of plain sight.

Most home inspections don't reveal much of anything, maybe faucets that need tightening, or caulking that needs to be done. The point of an inspection is not to convince you that so much is wrong with the house that you are discouraged to buy it. It is rather to give you an accurate depiction of the current condition of the house, as well as an idea of how certain things will hold up in the future.

When major items are found, such as a failing air conditioning unit, or bad wiring, the parties must look to the real estate contract to see who will be required to make the repairs. Home inspections typically cost anywhere from $200 and up, depending on the size of the home. After the inspection is complete you will be given a detailed report of all the inspector's findings, whether good or bad, usually accompanied by digital photos.

A typical home inspector will inspect the structural elements of the home consisting of the roof, outside and inside walls of the home, patios and driveways, as well as parts of the foundation if visible. They will go into the attic to inspect the trusses, the underside of the roof decking for water intrusion, and insulation. The systems of the home will be inspected including the electrical, HVAC, and plumbing systems. All appliances that are staying with the home are inspected and tested for proper operation, and usually a random spot check of electrical outlets, windows, and doors will be done.

Other items that a home inspection company might perform for additional fees include radon gas and mold testing, water analysis, and pool and spa inspections. Most home inspectors subcontract for a termite inspection that may be at an additional cost to you, but it is a very important part of any home inspection here in Florida. Ask your real estate agent, or friends and family for home inspection referrals.

"11th Month" Inspections

If you are buying a new construction home, the typical builder warranty period for materials and workmanship runs out after one year. (Structural and mechanical items are usually covered for longer).

Before the one-year anniversary of buying their home, a lot of people get what's commonly referred to as an 11th month inspection done by a qualified home inspector.

This is one last opportunity to identify and report any defects to the materials or workmanship in your home that you may not have previously discovered to the builder, and I highly recommend you do this.

Home Warranties

If you are buying a new home from a builder, one of the advantages you have is that your home will usually come with a warranty provided and paid for by the builder.

But this doesn't mean that you're out of luck if you decide to buy a resale home. There are several home warranty options available to you, no matter the age or condition of the home you are buying.

Home warranties for average homes under approximately 5,000 square feet will typically cost you between $400 and

$500 dollars per year. You can renew these on a yearly basis.

Most plans do not require an inspection of the property before they take effect. Depending on the company you choose and the specific plan you go with, an additional amount may be needed to warrant some items like the A/C, refrigerator, washer/dryer, and a pool or spa.

Typically covered items include the plumbing, electrical, and heating systems, water heater, most appliances, disposal, smoke detectors, and exhaust fans. You need to read the warranty contracts carefully to see exactly what is and what is not covered. For example, a warranty might cover your refrigerator motor, but not the shelving inside the refrigerator.

Should something that is covered by the warranty break down, there is usually a service call fee, anywhere between $50 and $100. Other than paying that, you will not be required to pay out any money for the repair or replacement of a covered item.

Most home warranties are pretty simple to acquire, fairly inexpensive, and are usually worthwhile. There are more than a dozen national home warranty companies to consider but here are two that I've known people to use:

American Home Shield

ahs.com

Old Republic Home Protection

orhp.com

CHAPTER TWENTY-THREE
NEW HOME CONSTRUCTION

FOR SOME RETIREES, building a new home in Florida is the ultimate dream. There's not much more exciting in real estate than picking a lot, choosing or designing a floorplan, making your interior design selections, and seeing it all come together right before your very eyes.

Besides being exciting, it can also be described as overwhelming, daunting, mind boggling, and a slew of other adjectives. After reading this chapter, you should feel comfortable enough with Florida new home construction that if you do choose to build a new home here, the words you use to describe it will hopefully lean more towards "exciting."

Choosing a Builder

There are many factors that should go into your choice of home builder. The most important factors are those that are important to you. Of course, these are different for everyone.

Some people want the very best price available, while others don't mind paying more for higher quality. Some want a builder that will hold their hand throughout the entire process, while others prefer to have very little contact with the builder. Others still want total control over their selections, while some don't mind if the builder even chooses the colors. It's very important that you decide for yourself what factors are important to you before you start looking for a builder.

Once you decide on the factors that are most important to you, do some investigating. If it's the best price you desire, visit several communities and see which builder is offering the best incentives. Builders with numerous homes in their inventory ready to move into are more likely to give incentives than a builder who has no standing inventory. Check the local paper in the area you are looking for homes, and scan the advertisements for good deals and incentives. A local real estate agent might be able to point you in the direction of the best deals in town.

If quality is the most important thing to you, spend some time in the builder's model homes looking around on your own and examining things like the trim work, the drywall, and the paint. Look for anything that's not quite right such as wavy walls or uneven paint applications. Chances are if the builder didn't take the time to get his models right, he won't take the time to get your home right. If the builder does not have a model, see if he has a list of customers that you may contact to try and go see their homes.

Working with the builder and his staff

The first person you will meet when looking at model homes will be the builder's sales staff. Start with them. Are they presentable, eager to help answer your questions, and polite? Or are they abrasive, pushy, rude, and uncaring? Typically, if they like their jobs, and take pride in the product they are representing, odds are good that you're looking at a pretty good builder.

Remember that the salesperson will typically be the direct line to the builder for you throughout the homebuilding process. Keep in mind that you are probably not their only customer. So if they are busy with others when you stop by to ask a question or report a complaint, be respectful of them and their time. Respect is reciprocal.

Some builders will have you meet with different members of their staff during different phases of the construction process. You may meet with a decorator, an architect, a superintendent, or all of these before and during the construction process. To save time for everyone, before meeting with each representative, have your questions ready.

A few builders allow their customers to walk the construction site whenever they want, others only allow it at specific times during the process. In either case the builder's insurance policy usually does not cover you if you are injured, if you step on a nail, or trip and fall over some plywood. Construction sites, no matter how well they are supervised can be dangerous; so most builders require that you be escorted by someone on their staff when you visit the construction site and that you visit at times when subcontractors are not working inside. It may not always be convenient or possible for you to get to the construction site during the builder's business hours. If that is the case, you are at your own risk when you visit the site.

How to Choose a Floor Plan

Obviously you need to choose a floor plan that fits well with the way you live your life. If you plan to use your home in Florida just as a second home or vacation home, and rarely expect to have many guests accompany you, then maybe a one or two bedroom condo, townhouse, or small home will fit your needs. If you expect more people, or plan to use the home as a primary residence and are accustomed to a much bigger home, obviously you will want to go bigger with a large condo (maybe even combine two adjacent units), a large townhouse, or a single family home.

The key to finding a floor plan that fits your needs is to spend some time in the builder's model homes, if available, and try to envision things such as furniture layouts, traffic patterns, blending of public spaces, such as the flow from the kitchen to the living room, as well as private spaces, such as bedrooms and bathrooms. Place most of your interest in areas that meet your lifestyle needs. For example, if you love entertaining, look for an extra large great room and maybe an open kitchen. If you plan on having lots of visitors--and remember everyone wants to come to Florida--then focus on bedroom sizes. You get the idea.

You may be accustomed to the split bedroom floor plan. These are popular in Florida as well. However, in some developments where the lots are narrower (such as 40, 50, or 60, feet wide) you may find that split bedrooms are rare. Not many builders have found a way to make an efficient split bedroom floor plan for those size lots.

Most people, however, find that once they are in a home with the bedrooms on the same side, that they don't really miss the split bedrooms all that much. Split bedrooms are great for families, especially with teenagers who like to crank up their stereos or play their drums. Having the secondary bedrooms on opposite sides of the house from the master bedroom provides parents more peace and quiet. But most people retiring to Florida or using their home as a second home don't have that problem and find that a non-split plan works just fine for them.

Choosing a Lot

The selection of a lot to build your home on is, for some people, even more important than choosing the floor plan or who builds your house. We all know the saying, "location, location, location."

Some people are very particular about their lot, as well they should be. The lot you choose will determine several things, such as the quality of view you will have, your level of privacy, your utility bills, the price, and your home's future resale value. Some people could care less what lot their home is built on, but taking everything into consideration, they certainly should.

In Florida, water views, be it the ocean, river, lake, or pond are the most coveted, followed by views of a golf course. As such, prices and premiums you will pay to look at these vistas are higher than say, a lot with a view of the interstate. Also, many people like to have their home back up to a conservation area, which assures them of privacy in that nothing can be built behind them, but this also usually comes at a premium.

Lot Premiums

Lot premiums are an additional charge that home builders and developers tack on to the price of a new home depending on where in the community a lot is located.

Basically, the way most new homes are sold these days is a builder will advertise their homes based on standard features and a "standard" lot, and anything they can use to justify an increase in price is a premium.

As you can imagine, the definition of "standard" varies widely.

According to an article from one of the top real estate consulting companies in the country, in Florida all but the worst lots in new home communities have premiums associated with them, some as high as 10% of the base price of a home.

What kinds of lots typically command a premium?

- Oversized lots
- Lots that back up to a preserve

- Lots that back up to private land
- Golf front lots
- Golf view lots
- Cul de sac lots
- Corner lots
- Waterfront lots
- Lakefront lots

Another way to think about it is, look at what one might deem the worst lot in a community, and consider that a "standard" lot. Anything better than that, will probably carry a premium.

Are lot premiums worth it? That all depends on how badly you want a particular lot and how much it is ultimately worth to YOU...not the builder or any potential future buyer.

With that said, can you recoup the cost you paid for a lot premium if you go to resell the home down the road? This boils down to how much of a premium you pay and what a future buyer is willing to pay.

House/Lot Orientation

Most people don't think about it but the lot you choose can also have an effect on your heating and cooling costs. On most homes, the majority of the windows are located on the front and rear of the home. If the home is placed on a lot with an east/west exposure (home faces east or west) more sunlight will enter the home, increasing your utility bills in the summer, and lowering your heating costs in the winter.

There are other considerations if you are going to have a swimming pool at your home. If the rear of your home faces east, your pool and patio areas will be shaded from the sun in the afternoons but will have the morning sun. Some people prefer the afternoon shade while some prefer the afternoon sun. Others still prefer a north/south exposure, which evens out the two extremes. There is no right or wrong answer, but you'd be doing yourself a disservice if you did not at least consider what you might like before choosing a lot. My advice is try to visit the lot you are considering at different times of the day and see what exposure you think will work best for you.

Making Your Selections

After finalizing your contract with the builder, you will be given a time to either meet with the builder's decorator, or to visit their design center. This is when you pick all the colors and interior materials that will give your home its personality, including things like cabinets, carpeting, tile, countertops, paint colors, and so on. Depending on the size home you've chosen, this may be a short two to three hour process, or it could span several appointments over the course of a couple days or weeks.

No matter how many homes you build, this will always be one of the most stressful times because what you choose here will determine how your home is going to look and function for years to come. To minimize the time and stress that picking everything out will invariably cause, it pays to have done your homework as to what you like beforehand. This way you won't be making any split second decisions on things that you might not be able to change later. Take pictures of ideas you see in model homes or tear out pictures in magazines of things you might like to have in your new home.

Critical Steps in the New Home Construction Process

Over the next several pages I'll cover the critical steps in the new home construction process to help ease your mind during what can be a confusing and frustrating time. While it won't by any means tell you how to go out and build your own home, this information should give you the knowledge to feel a bit more comfortable with everything that will go on during the new home construction process.

Permitting

Once the floorplan and other structural features of the home have been selected, the builder will submit the plans to the city for approval. When submitted, the plans for the home must usually be accompanied by an architect's or an engineer's seal, essentially stating that they certify that the home is planned in accordance with the proper design specifications and building codes. Hard construction cannot begin until the permits have been received back from the city.

If the city feels the plans submitted comply with all current zoning and building codes, they will issue the builder permits to build the home. A copy of the plans and permits will be kept in a permit box in plain view at the construction site and checked frequently by city inspectors throughout the construction process.

Fill, Compact, and Site Prep

Most of the residential lots being built on these days in Florida require at least some amount of fill dirt to bring them up to the elevation required by the city or municipality which issued the building permit. Usually once the lot is filled and compacted, an engineer will come out and conduct a compaction test, to make sure the dirt added to the lot has been properly compacted. Not every lot that is filled needs to be tested for compaction. The builder usually has a set standard for lots that they test, such as lots requiring more than one foot of fill. A lot that has not been compacted properly is prone to settling, which can cause cracks in foundations and walls, and more trouble for you down the road.

Anything else that stands in the way of construction of your new home will be removed at this point. Brush will be cut back. Trees too close to the home are susceptible to damage by trucks and other machinery, and tree roots can damage the foundation, so if any trees still need to be removed it will happen at this time. The lot will be graded, generally sloping slightly towards the front, back, and sides to help with drainage. The area of the lot where the home will go will also be leveled, so that in the end, your house will be level as well.

Hub and Tack

Once the lot is filled and compacted, a survey crew will come and stake out the home, also called hub and tack. At this point, the corners of your home will be set.

Form the Slab

Pieces of lumber, typically 2 x 10s turned on their side, are used to create the perimeter of the slab. Footers are then dug out underneath the 2 x 10s. Footers, which are a couple of feet deep (depths vary area to area and builder to builder), and wider than the walls of the home, provide the support necessary to help make the house more sturdy.

Metal reinforcements rods will run around the perimeter of the home and will be positioned vertically at certain intervals to go up inside of the block that will be placed on top of the slab. These will eventually help connect the slab to the tie beam at the top level of the block.

Elevation and Setback Survey

At this point, a survey is done to make sure that the home is being built within the confines of its particular lot, and does not encroach on neighboring properties. The elevation of the lot is also checked, to be sure that it is at the height required by the city, county or municipality that issued the permit.

Rough Plumbing and Inspection

Water and sewer lines, which will be in place under the foundation of your home, are run at this time. The water lines will typically be made of copper, and drainage lines will be made of PVC piping. Any electrical outlets needing to be placed in the floor can also be installed at this time. Otherwise the slab will have to be cut later to install them. Once complete, an inspector will verify that each element of the rough plumbing has been installed properly.

Termite Treatment

Most builders in Florida will provide some form of termite treatment for the home. The most common type is a slab pretreatment that will be done before the slab is poured. The purpose of this pretreatment is to prevent termites from getting into your home and doing serious damage in the future. If you were to visit your new home the day that it is treated for termites, you may be overcome by a very strong odor. That's the termite treatment.

Due to environmental, scheduling, and cost concerns, some builders will not pretreat your slab but will treat the actual wood inside your home. After the framing is complete you may see that it looks like the bottom three or four feet have been stained, usually a greenish color. In this case, a termite treatment such as Boracare® has been used to treat your home for termites. The jury is still out as to which is the better treatment for the prevention of termites.

Prep the Slab

Once the rough plumbing is completed, a vapor barrier comprised of several sheets of plastic will be placed over the area in which the slab will be poured. This helps to keep moisture in the ground from penetrating the foundation and getting into your home once the slab has been poured over it.

Slab Inspection

Before the slab is poured an inspector will come and make sure that all work done up until this point is up to code, that all procedures have been properly followed, and construction is safe to proceed.

A side note here about inspections. While absolutely necessary, they can add a significant amount of time to the construction of your home, especially in areas where there is a lot of construction going on. Inspection departments are notoriously understaffed and overburdened with work. Sometimes you may see your house just sitting idle, with no work going on and your natural reaction may be to get angry with the builder.

Believe me, the builder wants to complete your home quickly, sometimes more quickly than you may even want him to. While your home is under construction he is likely carrying costs such as a mortgage on the land, insurance, and taxes, not to mention hard construction costs. Understand that when your home is sitting idle that sometimes it is the builder experiencing delays, but most often he is probably waiting on an inspection to be completed before he can proceed.

Pour the Slab

Next, the slab and the footings are poured. In the case of a monolithic slab, one long continuous pour of concrete is all it takes to create your slab. Wire mesh, or more commonly these days, high strength fibers, are usually embedded in the slab to increase its strength and help minimize cracking.

Ideal weather conditions for the pouring of your slab are that the weather should be dry, with little to no chance of rain during the pour, and temperatures should not be extremely hot or extremely cold. If after the slab is poured, it appears rain may be in the forecast, sheets of plastic should be placed over the freshly poured slab to keep it from getting wet. Excess moisture can affect the appearance of the concrete, as well as the integrity of the slab.

While the slab won't reach its ultimate strength for 20 to 30 days, it will usually be strong enough for construction to proceed in just a few days.

Slab Cracks

Eventually with almost every concrete slab, you may see some hairline cracks. They most likely won't appear for a couple months but inevitably some will appear. These do not indicate that you have a bad slab, but are most likely just settling or expansion cracks, the result of extreme temperatures, wind, and evaporation of water in the concrete. One concrete company representative said that the only guarantee they can give is that all concrete will crack, it's just a matter of when and to what degree.

If you are overly concerned about cracks that have appeared in your concrete slab, you might request that the builder hire an engineer to come take a look and certify that it is okay. You will likely have to pay for this service, but if it helps you sleep better at night, it may well be worth the few hundred bucks.

Foundation Survey

Once the slab is in place, another survey will be conducted, just to be extra certain that your home will not encroach on anyone else's property. It's better to discover this problem at this stage, when it will likely cost only several thousand dollars to fix, rather than later when it's a much more costly problem to fix.

Block

It takes a few days for the slab to cure long enough to support block being placed on top of it. Once the slab is cured, the block is then placed on top of the slab to form the outside walls, or shell of your home. Holes are left where the doors and windows will go, and any glass block that you have ordered is normally installed at this stage as well.

You will also see holes every so often along the bottom row of block called inspection ports where the metal reinforcement rods are sticking up from the slab into the block. These holes are included so the inspector can see that the slab, by the use of the metal in it, is effectively attached at set intervals by metal and concrete to the block walls.

Solid Pour Cells, Lintels and Tie Beam

Steel and poured concrete will be added to the block at predetermined intervals, usually every four or five feet. This process is done to add extra strength to the shell of your home and as previously mentioned, connect the shell to the slab. Lintels around all windows and doors will be poured to add strength around these openings, and then the tie beam (top layer of block poured solid) will be poured. This will have steel rods embedded in it as well, and hurricane straps that will later be attached to the trusses will also be embedded in the tie beam.

Lumber and Roof Trusses Get Delivered

About this time in the construction process, your roof trusses and the lumber for your roofing and interior framing are usually delivered. In some cases these materials may sit unused for some time while other projects are being worked on. Just how long they sit out, exposed to the elements, rain, sunshine, and heat depends on the builder's efficiency in scheduling as well as availability of work crews. To minimize weather exposure most builders will at least cover the materials lying out with tarpaulins or plastic sheets.

Trusses and Roof Decking

Your trusses, which will arrive at the home site already assembled and ready to install, act as a sort of skeletal system for your roof. They will be set on top of the block usually with the assistance of a crane. Once they are secured to the block walls with the metal "hurricane" straps embedded into the tie beam, the roof decking will be placed on top.

OSB vs. Plywood

Some builders use plywood roof decking while others use oriented strand board, or OSB. There is endless controversy about which is the better product. The fact is though that both products are excellent in their purest, undamaged forms. The problem that sometimes occurs with OSB is that its exterior "seal" may get damaged on site and lessen its integrity and ability to repel water. Don't fret if your builder insists on using OSB; just make sure that each piece being placed on your roof is in good condition.

Framing

Framing of the interior walls of your home will also be done at this time, and rooms will really start to take shape. Don't worry too much if the framing work looks a little rough at this point. There will be a framing "punch-out" later where everything that needs correcting will be taken care of. Feel free to point out anything that you think may not be obvious to the builder, mistakes can and do happen, but also feel secure in knowing that there will be a framing inspection to make sure everything has been done safely and correctly. Some builders will also do a framing walkthrough with you just to make sure everyone agrees nothing has been overlooked.

Window Installation

Windows will be installed and usually any sliding glass doors in your home will be installed as well. You may notice that windows on some homes in Florida will be single glaze windows, also known as single-pane windows. If you are coming from a cooler climate you may be shocked at first that builders in Florida use single-pane windows, as you wouldn't have even thought of using them up north. However, single-pane windows are used quite frequently in Florida. One argument you'll hear some builders make is that Florida does not experience the wide temperature swings like the north does. Another argument for them is that it takes about 5-7 years of energy savings to recoup the cost of installing the double-pane windows versus the single-pane, while most people move every 4-5 years anyway. This doesn't mean you should necessarily settle for single-pane windows. If you plan on being in the home more than a few years, the investment will pay off for you.

With double pane windows the extra pane of glass and the air in between the two panes adds a few extra layers of insulation and therefore comfort to your home. Triple-pane windows are even available on some higher end homes.

Impact Resistant Windows

Impact resistant windows are also gaining in popularity with the increasing awareness of hurricanes and the damage they can cause. In fact, in more and more coastal areas, new homes that are in what is called the "wind-borne debris region" are required to have either impact resistant windows, or some other approved window covering or shutters. Shutters are often the prevailing choice of cost conscious builders and home buyers, as impact resistant windows can be very expensive; usually three to four times the cost of standard windows.

Roof Felt

A layer of felt-like material will be placed over the roof decking to provide an extra layer of moisture protection. If shingles get blown off in a storm, water still has the roof sheathing covered by this felt to contend with before it can enter your home.

Shingles

The shingles are now placed on the roof. The most common type of roof shingle on production homes are asphalt shingles because they are relatively inexpensive and they get the job done. Asphalt shingles will be nailed down to the roof. Asphalt shingles come in 5-year to over 50-year ratings. The higher the rating, the more substantial the shingles and thus the higher levels of winds they can withstand. The builders marketing materials will usually specify the rating of the shingles they install.

You should keep in mind that if you get, for example, a 30-year rated shingle, in all likelihood it will not last you 30 years. Florida's weather fluctuations from warm to sweltering and dry to wet, can take a heavy toll on roof shingles. The factory ratings are for the shingle's lifespan under ideal weather conditions.

Tile and Metal Roofs

Alternatives to asphalt shingles are tile, either made of clay or concrete, and metal roofs. Though each is more expensive than asphalt shingles they will both last longer and require a little less maintenance. The covenants in the neighborhood where your home being built will sometimes dictate what type of roof your home must have, but if given a choice, you might consider a tile or metal roof.

Tile roofs have a long lifespan if installed and maintained properly. Roof tiles are made in a variety of colors to blend with your home's specific design needs. Trusses must be engineered to hold extra weight as tiles weigh considerably more than asphalt shingles. Impact such as that caused by hail can break tiles, and you should have them inspected periodically for damage to prevent problems down the road. When installed properly, roof tiles are less likely than asphalt shingles to blow off in inclement weather.

Metal roofs are also gaining in popularity, partly due to the resurgence of the "Old Florida" architectural look, and also because of their durability. Some roofing companies are offering lifetime warranties for metal roofs, which is a very attractive feature. Metal roofs are also available in different colors to match your home's design. Though the metal material itself reflects the sun's rays, it has a low R-value because it is a conductor of heat, but dead air space and attic insulation can be utilized to increase energy efficiency. As you could probably imagine, noise can sometimes be an issue with rain or hail storms on metal roofs, but sound-deadening insulation can be used to mitigate this problem. Some metal roofs can become dented when hit by falling objects like hail, but some manufacturers offer a "no-dent" guarantee.

Plumbing Top Out

At this stage toilets and bathtubs will be set and the plumbing lines will be stubbed out. Tubs will usually be made of marble, fiberglass, or acrylic and this will be spelled out in the builder's marketing materials. Jetted or "whirlpool" type tubs are usually available, and are especially nice in master bathrooms. Tubs should be covered with either cardboard or plastic during the remainder of the construction process as they can easily be damaged by a dropped hammer or similar accident.

You usually have a choice between elongated or round toilets. Also, "comfort" commodes that are a few inches higher than standard toilets for "ease of use" are usually an option. Check to be sure that the tubs and toilets that are installed are the color and style you have selected.

HVAC Rough-In

HVAC, which stands for heating, ventilation and air conditioning, will be roughed in at this time. Your air ducts, air vents, and air returns, which regulate the temperature throughout your home, will now be installed. Each room should also have its own air return. This is important because air returns keep your home's air temperature balanced. In homes where this has not been done, you can often have as much as a ten degree difference in temperature from room to room.

Air Conditioner Size

Most people when comparing air conditioning units are overly concerned with tonnage, or how big the unit is. But in reality, the tonnage is something that has a point of diminishing returns, meaning that bigger isn't necessarily going to give you better results. The local building codes will dictate the size, or tonnage that the A/C unit used in your home should be, based on the size of your house. The size of what will be installed might also be spelled out in your builder's marketing materials or sales contract.

SEER Rating

Here's what is important. Your air conditioning unit will have what is called a SEER rating, or seasonal energy efficiency rating. Many older homes have A/C units with SEER ratings as low as 10. The higher the SEER rating, the better the performance (energy efficiency) of the unit. Most builders will let you upgrade the A/C unit so that you can get a higher SEER rating unit if you desire.

Electric Heat Pump

In all likelihood your heating system will be an electric heat pump, also not very popular up north. This system will use the same ducts as your air conditioner. Electric heat pumps are not very efficient in temperatures below freezing. At extremely low temperatures an electric heating element kicks in to help the system out. Up north that might be on constantly. But here in Florida, electric heat pumps are the most cost effective and efficient heaters you can have installed in your home. The temperature is rarely below freezing, allowing your heating system to run in its most efficient state most of the time.

Electrical, Phone, Cable and Security System Rough In

Now all of your electrical outlets, cable outlets, phone jacks, and the security system will all be wired in. There are certain minimum requirements for the number and spacing of electrical outlets. Most new homes far exceed these minimum requirements.

Smart Box

Usually located in the garage, utility room, closet or some other out of the way place in most new homes is what may be referred to as a smart box. The smart box is the central hub for all cable, phone, and high-speed Internet lines running into and throughout your home.

Outlet Locations

Well before this stage, preferably at the time of selections and before the builder submits for the permit if possible, you should let the builder know if you have any special outlet location requests. Otherwise, it will be a costly mess to have outlets moved or added later, when drywall has to be cut and removed to make any changes. Note that some builders will charge for this service and some will not agree to do it at all, but this is something you should ask about while shopping for a builder.

GFI Outlets

Special electrical outlets will be installed in your kitchen, bathrooms, laundry room, garage, and in any other indoor and outdoor locations where water might commonly come in contact with the outlet. These outlets, clearly marked GFI or GFCI for Ground Fault Circuit Interrupter, are safety devices designed to prevent electrocution.

At the first sign of trouble, such as water coming into contact with electricity, they are designed to shut-off or kick the breaker to that particular outlet and prevent you from being electrocuted. Make sure that whoever does your walkthrough with you, shows you how these operate and that they check to make sure that they are functioning properly.

Security Systems

One of the most popular options on new homes today is the security system. Whether for a personal residence or a part-time second home, it's nice to have the peace of mind that a security system can offer. The security system is typically comprised of a base unit where the system is controlled from; one or more motion detectors; and sensors placed on doors and windows that alert you if one of them is opened. Other accessories include glass breakage sensors and carbon monoxide sensors. Make sure that all of your home's smoke detectors are hard wired into the system, so that if one of them should detect smoke, you as well as the fire department, will be alerted. An intercom system can be integrated into most security systems, and video surveillance technology is also available at a much higher cost.

Exterior Doors

The exterior doors, such as the front door and any side exterior doors will now be installed. They can be made of solid wood or a wood composite, metal, or more commonly these days fiberglass. Fiberglass is extremely durable, less likely to dent than steel, and easy to paint.

Framing Punchout

As mentioned earlier, any last corrections that need to be made to the framing before inspection will be done at this point.

Framing, Electrical, Plumbing, and Mechanical Inspections

Next, a whole slew of inspections happen. Typically, you won't even be made aware of it if some aspect of the home fails inspection. But not to worry, the house will not proceed until everything that may be wrong with it has been corrected and re-inspected. Failed inspections happen, and it shouldn't give you the impression that you are getting a substandard home. You should be thrilled that someone has been careful and diligent enough to catch any mistakes, to prevent problems for you down the road.

Stucco

Stucco is now applied to the outside of the home, providing another layer of protection for your home to the elements. Stucco is basically a muddy mixture of cement, dirt, and water applied to the outside of the block walls of your home. Before the stucco can be applied to the house, a layer of sheathing and a wire lathe must be placed over any exterior wood framing, such as porch ceilings, to protect the wood and to help the stucco adhere. Blocks walls, however, can have the stucco applied directly to them.

Exterior Paint

Now the outside of the home will be painted the color you selected. Several builders in Florida, after having experienced never before seen water penetration through block walls during the tropical season of 2004, have started using elastomeric paint to help keep wind-blown rain from penetrating the outer shell of their homes.

It is highly recommended that you seek out a home builder using this type of paint, or have your home painted with it soon after you move in. The elastomeric paint is a "water-proofing" paint, not necessarily waterproof, that is applied and a factory representative will usually inspect the application to ensure that it was done properly.

Insulation

Different types of insulation will now be placed in different parts of your home. For example, very thin foil insulation will be placed inside the exterior block walls, batted insulation will be placed between the studs of some interior walls and-- if possible-- in parts of the ceiling. The remainder of the ceiling will have blown-in insulation, especially in those areas that are hard to reach. Thick, fire rated insulation will also be placed between the garage and the interior of the home to form a fire barrier.

R-Value

The effectiveness of the insulation to resist heat from entering the living areas of the home is measured in what is called an R-Value. In Florida, all builders and sellers of new construction homes are required to disclose to you what the R-value is of the insulation installed in the different areas of the home. This will most often be in your sales contract, but it could be under a separate "insulation addendum" to the contract.

Quick Note About Garage Insulation...

Some builders insulate the garage ceiling, and some do not. You should be able to find out from the builder's marketing materials whether or not they do it. If not, and you plan to spend any significant amount of time working in your garage, I suggest you pay a little more to have insulation installed over the garage. It can make a big difference in the comfort of your garage, especially during the hot summer months.

Insulation Inspection

Because insulation is such an important component in your home from both a safety and comfort standpoint, there will be an inspection to make sure the right type and right amount of insulation have been installed properly in the required places.

Soffit and Fascia

The soffit and fascia are aluminum or vinyl materials that are used to cover the eaves, or where the roof overhangs the outside walls of the house. The soffit is designed to prevent water and bugs from entering the home, while still allowing air to flow into and cool the attic.

Drywall

The interior walls of your new home in Florida will most commonly be constructed of drywall, also referred to as "wall board." The drywall will be nailed to the wood studs inside your home and the seams will be hidden by tape. The rooms of your new home are really taking shape now.

Drywall is typically less expensive and less durable than the plaster walls that you may have had or seen in older homes.

Drywall is available in different thicknesses, the most commonly used thickness being ½ inch thick. Thicker drywall is generally preferred because each increasing level of thickness adds extra insulating, durability, and sound deadening properties. Also, thicker drywall, especially 5/8 of an inch or thicker, is easier to hang pictures on than ½ inch drywall. Different types of specialized drywall are also available albeit at higher costs such as fire-rated drywall or sound deadening drywall. As with anything else, having the builder install thicker drywall or any specialized drywall will usually result in an increase in costs.

Over the first year or so in your new home, drywall cracks, and nail or screw pops may appear as the house is breaking in and going through a shrinkage process. Near the end of your initial warranty period, usually one year, you should have the builder repair these minor cracks and nail or screw pops.

Windowsills

After the drywall is installed but usually before it is textured, the windowsills will be installed. Most production builders these days are using cultured marble or solid surface windowsills, but some use real wood sills. Many experts prefer cultured marble or solid surface as opposed to wood because windowsills sometimes can get wet if you leave a window cracked open accidentally, and moisture and wood don't go well together.

Drywall Texture

Your drywall job will not be complete without a layer of texture applied to give it some depth, added durability, and also to help hide any imperfections. Two of the most common types of texture being applied in Florida today are called "knockdown" and "orange peel."

Knockdown texture can best be described as looking like splatter, while orange peel looks like--you'll never guess--the peel of an orange. Looking through the builder's model homes, speaking to the sales staff, or reviewing their sales literature will give you an idea of what types of texturing they use.

I briefly mentioned plaster walls before and if you prefer the look and feel of plaster, it can be applied to certain types of drywall. Just check with your builder for the ability to upgrade, and their willingness to do that for you.

Trim carpentry

At this stage a trim carpenter will go into your new home and install the baseboards, special moldings such as crown molding if offered by the builder, chair rails, and doorframes. Interior doors will also be delivered to the home around this time but won't be installed until after they are painted.

Interior Paint

Your inside painting will be completed at this time. Make sure to request that two coats of paint be applied. Don't fret if the paint does not look perfect at this point. There is still work to be done inside, and a final paint touch up will occur before your home is complete.

Most builders will offer you a choice of colors that you can choose from when you make your initial selections. Be aware though that some production builders do not allow you to choose, and only offer white. If this is the case, you'll either have to paint the interior of the home the colors you want yourself or hire someone to come in and do it for you.

One tip I can give you is that if you are hiring someone to do the work for you, they will usually quote you a lower price if there is no furniture for them to move or have to cover up. So if possible, have your new home painted before moving anything into the home.

Garage Door

Your garage door will be installed about this time. The garage doors for your home can be made of wood, fiberglass, or most commonly on production homes, steel. Garage doors are rated based on their "wind load" which is the amount of positive and negative pressure they can withstand.

Most people aren't aware that roughly 80% of hurricane damage to a home starts with wind entering through the garage. This makes the garage door the most vulnerable part of your home when it comes to hurricanes, so you'll want to make sure that the garage door on your home is sturdy and made to withstand high winds. This is usually accomplished with the use of heavier, sturdier door materials; door insulation; and many horizontal rows of steel bracing.

Specifications for your garage door were likely submitted with your house plans to the permitting office in order to certify that it is up to local code, and an inspector will verify that the proper door was installed when inspecting your home during construction. In most cases additional bracing can be added, just contact a garage door contractor in the area to come take a look and tell you what options might be available to you.

Tile

Ceramic tile is common in most high quality homes in Florida, at least in "wet" areas such as kitchens, bathrooms and utility rooms. Lower cost homes will substitute linoleum, which can be made to look like real tile. Available in different sizes, tile can be installed pretty much wherever you want, is extremely durable, and can be fairly inexpensive.

It can also be very expensive, depending on your tastes and where the tile is made. Imported porcelain tile from Italy will be more expensive than ceramic tile manufactured in the United States, but most untrained eyes won't be able to tell the difference. Another option in higher end homes is travertine marble. In the end, the tile you choose to have put in your home will be a reflection of your personal taste and budget.

A quality tile job will have grout lines of consistent size, and there will not be any high spots or low spots in the tiles. A good tile layer will employ the use of a level to ensure an even application with no high or low spots. Once you move into your new home it is recommended that you have your grout sealed, or do it yourself, to prevent stains. While the tile can easily be cleaned with water and a mop, grout is much tougher to get clean so it's best to protect it from the start.

Lay out and pour driveway and sidewalks

Now your driveway, front and back patio, as well as any sidewalks, will be laid out and formed up. Once they are formed, they will be inspected to ensure they are the correct size and shape. Assuming they pass inspection, these areas will be poured with concrete.

Final Survey

With all of the components of the home, structure, driveway, sidewalks, and patios in place, a final survey will be conducted to ensure all components are within the setbacks where they are supposed to be.

Irrigation System

Your irrigation system, which can be run off your main water system, a reclaimed water system, or a deep well, will be installed at this point. Be aware that with a well, there is a chance that if the well is not dug deep enough, high levels of sulfur in the water can discolor your exterior paint job over time. Typically, the deeper the well, the less paint discoloring sulfur will be present in the water, and proper depths of deep wells will vary from area to area.

The irrigation system is usually controlled by a timer box that can be manual or electronic, allowing you to set watering times, and setting the system to water certain days, while skipping others. Several Florida cities and counties are experiencing severe water shortages because of rapid growth and development, along with other factors. Therefore, restrictions on how often and when you are allowed to water your lawn are sometimes in place. Check with your city water department for more information on what restrictions might be in place in your area.

Landscaping

Any landscaping that is included with your home will be installed, following the installation of your irrigation system. Most builders include a basic landscaping package with your home, and some will give you the option to upgrade that package. Otherwise, you may want to add some more landscaping after you move in, since most basic packages can be pretty sparse.

Measure Cabinets

In the case of custom, or even semi-custom cabinetry, the cabinet company will measure for those shortly after the drywall is in. While some minor corrections to cabinetry can be made in the field, a quality cabinet company will rely on accurate measurements at this stage to build your cabinets to exact specifications.

Cabinets

Cabinets range from entry level laminate cabinets to a step higher with thermofoil cabinets, which are essentially vinyl-covered particleboard, to faux wood cabinet doors with plastic or particle boards drawers and shelves at a step higher, to all wood cabinets at the highest end. Maple, hickory, oak, and cherry are the most popular types of wood cabinets and various stains and glazing such as cinnamon or pecan can be applied to each.

Again, just like most of the other important selections going into your home, the cabinets you choose will be determined by your personal preferences and most definitely budget. Be sure to put a lot of thought into your cabinetry, because if you decide you don't really like it that much a few years down the road, it can be expensive to replace.

One simple way to save a little money without sacrificing design is to have upgraded cabinets installed in your kitchen, and have standard cabinetry installed in your bathrooms. This way, everyone can marvel at your beautiful cabinets in the place where most people tend to congregate, the kitchen.

Counter tops

Your kitchen countertops are one of the most used components of your new home. Your choices range from inexpensive yet functional laminates, to solid surfaces like Corian®, granite, and Silestone®. Again, just like other components in your home, the product you ultimately choose will be based on factors such as personal taste as well as budget. A laminate counter will usually arrive with your cabinets, while solid surface counters must be custom measured for after your cabinets go in. Because of this there is often a couple week delay between your cabinets being installed and the countertop installation.

Laminate

Laminate countertops are made in a variety of colors, patterns, and textures. Laminate countertops are among the least expensive countertops available, yet many laminate countertops resemble the look of higher priced counters at first glance. Laminate countertops are not as durable as solid surface counters and can be cut or scorched easily, so you'll need to always make use of a cutting board when working with knives, and hot pads when using hot pots or pans.

Corian®

Corian®, invented by DuPont, is one of the most popular countertops available today and with good reason. It is extremely durable, nonporous (this makes it stain resistant), and with over 100 colors available, it can be used in a number of creative applications. Something you might want to think about is that some people decide to transition their solid surface countertops into their bathrooms as well, something you may not typically want to do with laminates.

While Corian® is extremely durable, care should still be used when cutting or cooking. Its cost far exceeds that of laminate counters. A typical kitchen will cost a few thousand dollars as opposed to a few hundred with laminate, but with the proper care and precautions, it should last you a whole lot longer.

Granite

Granite is a natural stone, quarried in several locations around the world. Available in a vast range of colors and patterns, granite's use as a countertop surface is very popular, especially in higher-end homes. Because it is a natural stone, no two pieces will ever look exactly the same, allowing the homeowner to express their own sense of flair and uniqueness.

Being that it is a natural stone, granite is porous, and must be sealed regularly to prevent staining. Most experts recommend that this be done twice a year. Granite is known for its hardness and durability, but again, as is the case with other solid surfaces, it is not scratch or burn proof.

Silestone®

Silestone® is a nonporous solid surface material made mainly of quartz, the fourth hardest natural mineral. Harder and more durable than granite, Silestone® is scratch, stain, and scorch resistant. However, the manufacturer recommends that as with any other solid surface countertop, proper precautions against each of those be taken. Because it is nonporous, it does not need to be sealed like granite does.

Like each of the other countertop options, Silestone® is available in a variety of colors and patterns and can be used in a variety of ways.

Appliances Are Ordered

If you have not picked out your appliances by now, you better get started. At least some of them, like the range, dishwasher, and any built-in microwave or wall ovens will be delivered around this time. Your builder will usually have you go to visit their supplier to have you pick them out, otherwise you might be stuck picking out your appliances from a catalog which really makes it tough. Your final appliances-- refrigerator, washer and dryer-- will usually come a little later.

Appliances might be one of the hardest items to pick out. You should do a lot of looking around at different makes and models before you decide. Appliances are usually available in white, black, bisque, or stainless steel. You should choose a color that coordinates with the rest of your kitchen.

Plumbing Trim

This is when your faucets will be installed. Popular finishes include polished or antique brass, chrome and nickel. You will most likely have picked out the type and style of fixtures you want at your appointment with the builder's decorator.

Mirrors and Shelving Installed

Your bathrooms mirrors get installed around this time. Mirrors range from standard flat mirrors, to more upscale beveled mirrors available in a variety of shapes. Some builders offer you a choice at your design meeting and some do not. If not, you can always have them changed out later.

Also, closet shelving, which is usually wire shelving in production homes, will now be installed. Some builders are offering the choice to upgrade to California® type closets, which provide a more useful and appealing shelving and hanging system customized to fit your needs. If your builder does not offer this but you just have to have it, once you move in just look up "closets" in the phone book and get some estimates.

Electrical and HVAC Trim

Your outlet covers and light switches will be installed, along with any light fixtures you have chosen for your home. Also, your air conditioning vents and return vents will be installed if they have not been already.

Attic Insulation

You might recall that when the insulation was installed, certain areas of your home's ceiling may have gotten batted insulation. At this stage the rest of your home's ceilings will get insulated with blown-in insulation. A large tube or hose runs from an insulation truck and the installer climbs into the attic and "blows-in" the rest of the insulation. They will usually apply it until there is at least a foot or more of insulation covering all areas.

Flooring

Any hardwood flooring or carpet you have requested will be installed at this time. You will have picked out your flooring choices at your meeting with the decorator, and now you get to see how it finally looks installed in your new home. If you're not excited yet, you should be. You're almost home!

Final Inspection

This is the last city inspection that your home will have. After it is complete, and assuming your home has passed, the city will then issue a Certificate of Occupancy (or "C.O." in builder-speak), basically stating that the home is habitable and has been inspected to meet or exceed local building standards.

Paint Touch-Up

The painter will go back in and touch up any spots he might have missed, or areas that have been scuffed, nicked, or otherwise damaged as things have been delivered and installed and people have been working.

Meter Installed

Up until this point, your home has been running on temporary power. Now the local power company will come out, remove the temporary power pole, and install an electric meter. A power company employee will check this meter each month to see how much power has been used, and the power company will use this information to calculate your bill.

Hot Check

With the home running on permanent power, all of the electrical functions of the home will be tested to make sure there are no shorts in the system, and make sure everything functions the way it should.

Install the rest of the appliances

With 99 percent of the work on your home complete, your final appliances will usually be delivered and installed. You will have a chance very soon at your final walkthrough to verify that these are in no way damaged, and that they work like they should.

Punch-out

Here the last one percent of work, which is often the most important, will be attended to. Either the superintendent or a walkthrough specialist will walk through your home examining it for quality finish and attention to detail. Anything out of order or not in tip-top shape will be taken care of.

Final Cleaning

After all construction work is done, a cleaning crew will go through the home cleaning it from top to bottom, mopping floors, vacuuming carpet, scrubbing toilets, and cleaning counters. After the cleaning it may be found that certain counters or tubs have been scratched during construction. If this is the case, they will be buffed or otherwise repaired.

CHAPTER TWENTY-FOUR
SWIMMING POOL
CONSTRUCTION

SOME OF YOU buying a home in Florida will have a swimming pool built along with your new home or put in once your home is finished. Here is how the process of building your pool will generally go.

First you will meet with the pool builder to go over all that you want in your pool. Visit several pool websites, buy some pool magazines and talk with other pool owners to get an idea of what you want. You'll need to decide on the size, the shape, the depth, where steps and ledges will go, waterfalls, spas, heaters, special jets, tile, interior coating (marcite) colors, and more.

The builder will submit plans for your pool to the city and wait to get the approved permit back before beginning. Once approved, the pool builder will lay out your pool according to the shape you requested and the city approved.

A backhoe will be used to dig out the pool, a truck will haul off some of the dirt, and some will be left to backfill and grade the pool deck later. Steel rebar will be placed in the pool to form a sort of "basket" in the shape of your pool.

At this point, drains, jets, and other plumbing will be installed. The city will inspect that the steel and pre-plumbing have been done up to code.

Then, fast drying, high strength concrete will be applied to create the shell of your pool. This process is called "shooting" the pool because the concrete is shot out of a hose. It actually looks like a pool now.

The excess dirt from digging the pool will be used to fill in around the outside of the shell and to grade the deck. Tile that you chose will be installed around the perimeter of the pool at this time.

Electricity is run to the pool equipment location and the equipment may also be installed around this time. The electrical work will be inspected as well as the plumbing lines. Assuming all is working well, the pool deck will be poured. Once the concrete dries it will be textured and coated with an acrylic type coating, which should last you several years with proper care.

Your screen enclosure, which usually requires a separate permit to ensure proper engineering and strength, will be done at this time. Now, the interior of your pool will be cleaned out and acid washed. It has probably had standing water, dirt, and construction debris in it, but no longer. The interior pool surface, most commonly a material called marcite is applied.

Your pool is filled almost immediately afterwards. Once filled, your pool builder will start-up and clean the pool and add the proper chemicals.

After you've been given your "new pool owner" orientation, you are ready to enjoy your pool. Some people prefer to maintain the chemicals in and clean their own pools, while others prefer to hire someone to take care of it.

My advice is to leave it to an expert, especially at the beginning. During the first few months of operation your pool goes through a "breaking-in" period and an expert can best control and guide this process. Once all the chemicals and the "mood" of your pool stabilize, you can take over the duties if you wish.

CHAPTER TWENTY-FIVE
NEW HOME WALKTHROUGH

THE WALKTHROUGH, or new home orientation as it is sometimes called, is one of the most important phases in the construction of your new home. It is a time for you to meet with the builder and let him or his representatives acquaint you with your new home and all of its components. The walkthrough is also a time for you to give your new home the once over, looking for any construction issues not up to quality standards. Here is what could be considered the ideal walkthrough in detail.

Allow Enough Time

Allow ample time to go through your new home. In my experience an hour and a half to two hours is sufficient for average sized new homes. Also, leave any pets, kids, or curious friends and relatives at home. There will be plenty of time for them to experience and enjoy your new home in due time. The walkthrough is serious business and should be treated as such. Minimizing distractions is critical.

What to Bring

To ensure a successful walkthrough bring along several pens or pencils, a black permanent marker, a packet of neon green dots available at office supply stores, a pad of legal paper, some bottled water, a digital camera (you probably have one on your phone) and a ton of patience. Understand that everything might not be perfect once you start the walkthrough. It's just the nature of home building that no matter how careful, the builder can't catch everything. But, if you follow my advice, the builder and his employees will be in the position to get things corrected for you in a timely fashion.

The order of the walkthrough is not really important as long as everything gets covered. As you find items not up to standards, place one of the neon green stickers I suggested you bring on the item and write it down on your legal pad or a "punchlist" provided by the builder. Then snap a quick picture of the problem. Green dots can mysteriously disappear but if you write it down and take a photo it can't be forgotten for long.

Breaker Box and Electrical System

You will of course be tempted to head for the front door and bask in the glow of your fresh new home. But not so fast. Let's cover some things in the garage first. The garage houses several important components of your new home and you should become familiar with them. The first item on the list is the breaker box. This is where the electricity that comes into your home is regulated. The walkthrough representative should show you where it is and how to operate it.

Make sure that each breaker has been clearly labeled for you. This will eliminate headaches down the road. Also, there should be some GFI outlets in the garage. Now is a great time for the walkthrough representative to test those in front of you, and to show you how they work. Also, make sure they test the GFI outlets inside the home when you get in there.

Hot Water Heater

Be sure to check the hot water heater. Make sure the size, measured in gallons, is what you contracted for. The walkthrough representative should show you how to turn it off so you will know how to when necessary. There are timers available for your hot water heater that can easily be installed that will save you some money on your electric bills. If your hot water heater comes with a timer, have the walkthrough representative show you how to set it.

Water Shutoff

The main water shutoff valve to the home will usually be located inside the garage or sometimes on the outside. The walkthrough representative may advise you to turn the water off if you will be leaving the home for days at a time. This is probably good advice, at least initially until you've lived in the home a while and made certain there are no leaky toilets or pipes.

If you do turn off your water, make sure that you also turn off the breaker for the hot water heater. The hot water heater has coils inside that can burn up if there is no water passing through. When you return home, it is very IMPORTANT to make sure you turn the water back on before turning the hot water heater back on.

Air Handler and Air Filter

The air handler, which distributes the heated or cooled air throughout your home, will usually be in the garage as well. Make sure the walkthrough representative opens the filter door to show you how to change the air filter. Using the black permanent marker, make note of the filter size in a conspicuous place on the front of the air handler. You should change the air filter about every month for best performance.

Garage Door

While you're still in the garage, open and close the garage door to check for proper operation and make sure the remote controls work. If your garage door opener came with an outside keypad, ensure that it too works. In the event of a power outage you may need to open the garage door manually. Have the walkthrough representative show you how to do that.

Kitchen

Once inside the home, the best place to usually start is the kitchen because there is so much to cover there. Make sure that there are no scratches on the kitchen countertops or cabinets. Open and close a random selection of cabinet doors to make sure they are working properly. Make sure the hinges are tight, and the cabinets aren't sticking or rubbing against anything as you are opening and closing them. The representative should give you care and cleaning instructions for both your counters and your cabinets.

Turn on the kitchen faucet and set it to the hottest setting. Here we are checking to make sure that the hot water heater is working properly. As long as you've got hot water after what you feel is a reasonable length of time, you're doing just fine. Have the walkthrough representative show you how the sink disposal works, and how to clear it if it gets clogged. Also have them show you where the individual shutoff valve is for the water in the kitchen as well as the locations of the GFI outlets.

Appliances

Examine the appliances that came with your home. First, examine the outside of them to make sure there are no scratches or dents. Accidents do happen during construction, but assuming you bought new appliances, and not scratch-and-dent specials, they should be in brand new condition. Turn the stovetop on, check that the burners are working, and then try heating the oven. Assuming everything is working thus far, start the dishwasher to run through a cycle. This is to mainly make sure that there are no leaks in the dishwasher, either when it fills or when it drains.

While the dishwasher is running do a quick check of the refrigerator. If there are integrated ice and or water controls in your refrigerator make sure they work. Don't use the first batch or two of ice; just discard it in the sink. Also, most manufacturers suggest running through and pouring out the first couple of gallons of water from the refrigerator. This is to make sure that the water line becomes clear of any debris that may have gotten inside during construction and installation.

If your home came with a microwave, also check to make sure it works. In the laundry room, start both the washer and the dryer if provided and make sure they are working correctly. Make sure the dryer vent hose is connected.

All of the appliance instructions and warranty information should be kept in one easy-to-access location. Some of them may have cards for you to fill out and mail in to the manufacturer to record your warranty.

Drywall and Flooring

Before leaving the kitchen, examine the flooring for quality. Also check the walls for any drywall imperfections and check the paint for any spots the painter may have missed. As you see things that don't meet your standards, write them down on the list and place a green dot on or near the problem area. This is so that the drywallers or painters know exactly where to look to correct the problem areas.

Continue your flooring and wall inspection throughout the remainder of the home. Don't forget to look up every now and then and inspect the ceilings.

Systems and Components

As you are going through the home, have your representative show you how various things work, such as how to set and control the thermostat, how to use the security system and intercom if there is one, and how to operate the central vacuum if you bought one. If your home has a fireplace, whether it is wood burning, gas, or electric, have the walk-through representative show you how it works. Make sure you are given instruction booklets on each of these items and that you place them with your appliance booklets.

Bathrooms

Visit the bathrooms and check that the plumbing works. Again turn on the hot water, then the cold water to check the functioning of each. Be sure to check the showers and baths, as well as the sink. Water lines sometimes get reversed. Hot will be cold, and cold will be hot, but this can be easily corrected. Flush the toilets and make sure they have adequate water flow and don't remain running long after you flush. Check the tile work inside the showers to make sure that there are no holes or gaps in the grout or caulking. You don't want water getting behind your tile in there. Examine the vanity tops for scratches and cabinets for loose hinges.

Exterior

Be sure to inspect the outside of your home as well. The walk-through representative should familiarize you with where the hose bibs are located, the sewer cleanout, the A/C unit and anything else that is important. Make sure all of the exterior walls of the home are evenly painted, and do an inspection from ground level of the roof to make sure there are no shingles that look loose or out of place. If your home comes with a sprinkler system, you should be shown how to operate that.

Warranty Information

After you feel you've examined the home top to bottom and have made note of anything that is not satisfactory, you should have the walkthrough representative go over any warranty paperwork that is given to you, so you have an understanding of what items in the home are covered and for how long. Most warranty plans cover most everything for a short period of time, usually the first year. The systems of the home, things like plumbing, electrical, and HVAC, will be covered for a little bit longer, maybe up to two or three years.

There will also be a warranty on the structure. This is the longest lasting component of the warranty. When you hear a builder say a ten-year warranty or 15-year warranty, they are referring to the warranty on the structure. The structure is usually deemed to include the foundation and footings, beams, lintels, columns, walls, roof framing systems and flooring systems.

When things settle down a little bit and you have some time, it can never hurt to read over all of the warranty information. This will help you feel more comfortable with the warranty claim and repair process should you ever need to go through it in the future.

Emergency Information

The walkthrough representative will usually give you a list of subcontractors who worked on your home so you can call them if you have a problem with something. You should also be sure that you have a list of repair people to contact should an emergency arise on a weekend or during any non-business hours.

These people should include the heating and A/C contractor should the heat or air break; the electrical contractor if you lose power due to something other than a loss of overall power from the power company; the plumber for if your hot water heater breaks or if there is a sewer stoppage; and finally the number for the roofer if you get a roof leak. I also recommend having the number for a 24-hour water extraction company handy, just in case a pipe breaks or a water heater bursts and your home is flooded.

Write all of these numbers down on one piece of paper and tape them to the inside of a cabinet so that you can find them easily in an emergency.

Sign Here Please

To conclude the walkthrough, the walkthrough representative will typically have paperwork for you to sign stating that he walked you through and familiarized you with everything in the home, and that all the workmanship was satisfactory. Just make sure that the items you found to be unsatisfactory are either on this paperwork or will be attached to it in some form or fashion.

It is not absolutely critical that these items all be completed before your closing, so long as they are documented as needing repair. Invariably in the days and weeks after you move in, you will find more items needing the builder's attention. Just write all these items down as you find them and bring them to the builder's attention.

It has been a long process but now you are all set to enjoy what you have longed for, a beautiful new home in Florida!

THERE ARE BASICALLY two places where real estate closings take place in Florida. The first and most common place is at a title insurance company, and the second is at an attorney's office.

Title Insurance Companies

Because of their importance in your real estate transaction, most title insurance companies provide closing services. It is very common for closings on property in Florida to take place at a title insurance company office. The title insurance company will act as a neutral third party to ensure that all terms of the contract have been met, and they will collect and disburse funds according to the terms of the contract.

What is Title Insurance?

Before your closing, a title insurance company will conduct extensive research into public records, surveys, and other recorded documents to ensure that no party (other than the seller) holds an interest in or has a lien upon the property you are trying to purchase. According to the American Land Title Association, nearly one-third of all title searches reveal a problem with the title. Unknown heirs, divorces, tax liens, and fraud or forgery can cause title problems. Thankfully most can be resolved before your closing.

Upon completion of their research, the title insurance company issues an owner's policy to the buyer, and a lender's policy to the lender. The seller will customarily pay for an owner's policy but, as with most other costs, this is negotiable. If you do end up having to pay for it, the cost will be $5.75 per $1,000 up to $100,000, and $5.00 per $1,000 thereafter. If you are financing, your lender will require you to pay for the lender's policy, but this does not cost very much. It will usually be only a couple hundred dollars or less because you are getting what's called a simultaneous reissue credit with the owner's policy.

Attorneys' Offices

Many states require that an attorney conduct the real estate closing, but that's not the case here in Florida. Even so, many people prefer the peace of mind that an attorney can bring to a real estate transaction. If your closing is being held at an attorney's office, it will most likely be the seller's attorney, since they usually pay for the title insurance policy. If that is the case, make sure that your attorney gets a copy of what you will be signing and has a chance to review it before you go to the closing. It is not critical for your attorney to attend the closing. Often times your real estate agent will attend as a courtesy to you, just be sure to ask.

Typical Closing Costs

There are costs other than the sales price that are incurred in every real estate transaction. As the buyer, your share of these costs will typically range from 1% to 2% of the sales price. The closing costs that you pay will be a function of a couple factors including what you have negotiated in the real estate contract and whether or not you are getting a mortgage. Costs that are customarily paid for by the buyer include:

- Recording of the deed
- Documentary stamps on the deed* ($.70 for every $100 of the sales price).

*This is typically paid by the seller in a resale transaction, but I included it here because many builders require the buyer to pay this

- Documentary stamps on the mortgage ($.35 for every $100 financed)
- Intangible tax on the mortgage ($.002 times the mortgage amount)
- Lender's title insurance policy
- Taxes
- Prepaid interest
- Prepaid HOA Dues, capital contributions, or transfer fees
- One year of insurance in full

- Appraisal Fee
- Underwriting Fee
- Flood certification fee
- And potentially more, depending on your unique situation and where you buy!

CHAPTER TWENTY-SEVEN
FLORIDA RESOURCES

POPULATION AND GROWTH

Over the last ten years, Florida's population grew by 14.6 percent, going from 18.8 million residents in 2010 to 21.5 million residents in 2020.

One of the best ways to mentally grasp the geographical distribution of Florida's population is to look at Florida's most populated areas. Distributed around the coastal areas and Central Florida's east-west corridor, more than three quarters of the state's population live in and around 10 major core based statistical areas:

1. Miami/Fort Lauderdale/Pompano Beach - 6,166,488
2. Tampa/St. Petersburg/Clearwater - 3,194,831
3. Orlando/Kissimmee - 2,608,147
4. Jacksonville - 1,559,514

5. North Port/Bradenton/Sarasota - 836,995
6. Cape Coral/Fort Myers - 770,577
7. Lakeland/Winter Haven - 724,777
8. Deltona/Daytona Beach/Ormond Beach - 668,365
9. Palm Bay/Melbourne/Titusville - 601,942
10. Pensacola/Ferry Pass/Brent - 502,629

Getting Around Florida

Florida is a lot bigger than most people think. The distance top to bottom is 447 miles, and 361 miles side to side. Florida is the twenty-second largest state, with 58,560 square miles. Florida's longest river is the St. John's River, which is 273 miles long. Lake Okeechobee is its biggest lake at 700 square miles, making it the second largest freshwater lake in the continental United States, ranking just behind Lake Superior.

Air Travel

Getting to Florida by air is pretty easy, no matter where you are going in the state. Florida currently has 16 international airports, with Orlando International Airport and Miami International Airport being the two busiest. Florida also has several regional and community airports which can be a good choice for avoiding long lines and big crowds at larger airports, assuming you can get flights to where you need to go.

Florida's Primary Commercial Service Airports (with Airport Codes)

- Daytona Beach International Airport (DAB)

- Destin–Fort Walton Beach Airport (VPS)
- Fort Lauderdale/Hollywood International Airport (FLL)
- Gainesville Regional Airport (GNV)
- Jacksonville International Airport (JAX)
- Key West International Airport (EYW)
- Melbourne Orlando International Airport (MLB)
- Miami International Airport (MIA)
- Northwest Florida Beaches International Airport (Panama City) (ECP)
- Orlando International Airport (MCO)
- Orlando Sanford International Airport (SFB)
- Palm Beach International Airport (PBI)
- Pensacola International Airport (PNS)
- Punta Gorda Airport (PGD)
- Sarasota-Bradenton International Airport (SRQ)
- Southwest Florida International Airport (Fort Myers) (RSW)
- St. Petersburg/Clearwater International Airport (PIE)
- Tallahassee International Airport (TLH)
- Tampa International Airport (TPA)
- Vero Beach Regional Airport (VRB)

Major Interstates

Florida's major interstate highways are I-95, I-75, I-4, and I-10. They primarily connect the state north to south and east to west.

I-95, which runs up and down the east coast of the United States, reaches Florida north of Jacksonville, and runs the length of the east coast of the state, ending in Miami. It meets with I-10 in Jacksonville, and I-4 in Daytona Beach.

I-75 connects the west coast of Florida with the Midwest states, making cities on the west coast, including Tampa, Sarasota, Bradenton and Naples, hotbeds for Midwest vacationers, second homeowners, and retirees. I-75 begins in Florida about 45 miles west of Jacksonville. Once it snakes its way to the west coast of the state, it passes through Tampa (where it meets up with I-4), Bradenton, Fort Myers, and finally Naples. Here it begins to run east-west to Fort Lauderdale.

I-4 runs through the central part of the state, connecting Tampa, on the west coast, with Daytona Beach on the east coast.

I-10 runs the width of the Panhandle of Florida and connects Pensacola with Jacksonville. If you were to keep driving west out of Florida on I-10 you would eventually end up in the Pacific Ocean near Santa Monica, California.

Toll Roads

Every year, it seems like more toll roads open up, and even some roads that previously did not have any tolls, become toll roads. The rates for tolls vary by area, but the easiest way to deal with tolls here in Florida is to get a Sun Pass or E-Pass, which operate through electronic stickers or portable devices you'll attach to the inside of your windshield, and this is connected to a pre-paid online account that you fund with a credit or debit card.

When you approach a toll area, you'll see lanes designated for SunPass and you'll drive through there and it will deduct the amount of the toll from your account. You can get more information about this at: sunpass.com

If you are in Central Florida, something else you might see signs for that's similar is E-Pass, the difference being E-Pass is owned and operated by the Central Florida Expressway Authority (CFX) and SunPass is owned and operated by Florida Department of Transportation. You can get more information at: cfxway.com

The important thing to know is SunPass works where E-pass is accepted and vice-versa. But if you plan to drive all over Florida, you should look into these two options. Both offer discounts on the posted toll rates (amount varies) and will save you bunch of time waiting in line at the toll booth.

Road Construction

In a continuing effort to prepare the state's roadways and interstates for Florida's growth, road construction projects are always underway. If you'd like to find out where they are located before making a trip, visit the Florida Department of Transportation online at: fdot.gov.

There you can also find other valuable information such as the mileage between major cities and the locations of Florida's rest areas, toll roads, and speed limits.

Speeding

Don't speed. The Florida Highway Patrol and other law enforcement agencies are the butt of jokes such as: "Welcome to Florida, may I have your license and registration please." Be aware that speeding fines are doubled in work zones in Florida. Speeding might leave you with a couple hundred bucks less to spend on your new home here.

511 Traffic Info

Florida offers an in-state travel information system that you can access by dialing 511 from a cell phone or landline. From 511, you can get updates on traffic for major roadways and interstates, as well as construction information, lane closures, and special alerts. The system is also available online at fl511.com

Florida Driver's License

If you'll be moving to Florida full time, you'll want to get a Florida driver's license. You can get that process started at the Florida Department of Highway Safety and Motor Vehicles website at flhsmv.gov

Save time getting your license by taking advantage of online appointment scheduling. After you get a Florida license, in most cases, you can renew online or by telephone.

Some retirees moving to Florida will be bringing their elderly parents to live with them, many of whom will continue to drive in their seventies, eighties and nineties. The state of

Florida offers a great resource covering many aspects of elderly driving at:

flhsmv.gov/driver-licenses-id-cards/florida-granddriver

Community Service

The volunteer rate for retirees is the highest of any age group. Invariably when you are ready to move to Florida, it will not be your parent's retirement with time spent solely on the golf course, napping in a hammock, or playing bingo every day. You are likely to want to spend at least part of your time volunteering for a worthy cause. Luckily, there are plenty of opportunities for you to get involved in community service in Florida. Whether you choose to help out at a local school part time, join the local chapter of the Red Cross or United Way, or help build homes for Habitat for Humanity, your time and experience will be highly valued and appreciated.

As you probably already know, you'll feel great about yourself for doing it. Getting involved in volunteer work naturally increases your quality of life. Many volunteer agencies actively seek out older volunteers for their expertise and availability.

For more information on volunteer opportunities visit volunteerflorida.org for more information on the Governor's Commission on Volunteerism and Community Service.

Health Care

Just over 20 percent of Florida's population is over age 65. This is the highest percentage of all states, and almost 50 percent higher than the U.S. average. Consequently, there are more than 250 hospitals in Florida, some of which are regarded as being among the best in the nation. You can be assured that there are cutting edge facilities close by, no matter which part of the state you move to.

According to U.S. News and World Report 33 meet high U.S. News standards and are ranked in the state.

Check out the U.S. News Best Hospitals Report for Florida here:

health.usnews.com/best-hospitals/area/fl

VA Medical Facilities

A high percentage of people moving to Florida have served in the military and are entitled to health care benefits from the Veteran's Administration. There are several VA Hospitals and Clinics throughout the state as well as VA Outpatient facilities located near most major cities.

For a complete list of VA hospitals, clinics, and outpatient facilities in Florida visit:

va.gov/directory/guide/state.asp?STATE=FL&dnum=ALL

Arts and Cultural Activities

If you're into the arts, cultural events, and festivals, Florida will not disappoint you. There are more than 340 museums, more than 30 theatre companies, more than 200 outdoor festivals, and countless galleries and craft shops dedicated to the Arts. Most major Florida cities have symphony orchestras. The addition of theme parks, and world-class beaches and state parks means that there is no reason for you or your visiting kids and grandkids to ever be bored. In fact, there is so much to do in all parts of Florida that they should be begging to come visit. And because the weather is so nice, most of these places and events can be visited and enjoyed year round.

Museums

For a comprehensive list of museums in Florida, visit the Florida Association of Museums website at:

flamuseums.org

Beaches

When one's thoughts turn to Florida, the first image that comes to mind for many people is a beach: white sand, gentle breeze, and the hypnotic sounds of the lapping of the waves. Ah, this is why we live here. Florida has more than 1,100 miles of coastline, the majority of that being white sandy beaches bathed in glorious sunshine for you to enjoy. Each beach in Florida is unique, and you are sure to enjoy visiting several different beaches around the state to see which is your favorite. Whether your pastime is surfing, boating, kayaking, or just floating around, you're sure to find a beach that fits your mood close by.

Regardless of where you choose to settle down, there is likely to be a great beach within driving distance. Here are some of Florida's best beaches:

floridaforboomers.com/beaches/

Beach Safety Tips

I feel it's important for me to remind all of my readers, especially those who might be making the move to Florida in the near future and who might have varying levels of ocean-going experience to use extreme caution, especially when the ocean is rough. Here are some tips to help keep you, your family, and friends safe.

Whenever possible, swim at a lifeguard-protected beach. Pay attention to beach warning flags and know what the colors mean. Obey all instructions and orders from lifeguards. Lifeguards are trained to identify hazards. Ask a lifeguard about the conditions before entering the water. This is part of their job.

Learn how to swim in the surf. It's not the same as swimming in a pool or lake.

Also, never swim alone. This is tough for people who consider themselves strong swimmers to understand. Swimming in the ocean is nothing like swimming in a pool or lake. The problem, no matter how rough the ocean may be, is people tend to be overconfident and throw caution to the wind. The ocean definitely takes some getting used to, so take it easy until you get used to swimming in it.

Rip Currents Are The Primary Culprit

Rip currents are channels of fast-moving water that can pull even the most experienced swimmers from shore. Here are 6 things to remember if you are caught in a rip current:

1. Remain calm to conserve energy and think clearly.
2. Never fight against the current.
3. Think of a rip current like a treadmill that cannot be turned off, which you need to step to the side of.
4. Swim out of the current PARALLEL to the shoreline. When out of the current, swim at an angle -away from the current–towards shore.
5. If you are unable to swim out of the rip current, float or calmly tread water. When out of the current, swim towards shore.
6. If you are still unable to reach shore, draw attention to yourself by waving your arm and yelling for help.

Don't Be Victim #2

Many people drown while trying to save someone else from a rip current. Don't be the second victim!

Instead, get help from a lifeguard. If a lifeguard is not available, have someone call 9-1-1. Throw the rip current victim something that floats–a lifejacket, a boogie board, a cooler, or an inflatable ball. Yell instructions on how to escape.

I hope you will take my advice to heart and be extremely careful when enjoying our beaches and oceans here in Florida.

Theme Parks

There's perhaps no better way to spend quality time with your kids and grandkids when they come to Florida than to visit one of the many theme parks that Florida has to offer. Most of Florida's theme parks are located in central Florida, making them easy to get to from almost anywhere in the state. There are a few things you need to know, however, before you go.

Price of Admission

Admission prices change frequently, though you are easily looking at over $100 for two people at most of the parks listed below. Discounts are usually available for Florida residents, senior citizens, members of the military, AAA members, and young children. Annual passes are also available and can provide good savings if you plan to visit a park several times a year. Visit the parks' websites for current admission prices and information on any discounts currently available.

When Not To Go

The best times to avoid the theme parks are during the summer, spring break, or winter break when millions of kids are out of school and family vacations are underway. Nothing's worse than waiting in line for hours on end in 95 degree heat, packed in with thousands of people, especially when you are seemingly the only person there who remembered to apply deodorant that morning. Also, try to steer clear of most major holidays. If you plan to live in Florida at least part time or visit frequently, this still leaves you with plenty of time to enjoy the theme parks at times when they are less crowded.

Parks

The Florida Park Service, managed under the Florida Department of Environmental Protection, runs one of the largest park systems in the country with 159 parks spanning more than 723,000 acres and 100 miles of beaches. Activities available for you to enjoy include swimming, diving, or snorkeling in Florida's rivers and springs, bird watching, fishing, and hiking on scenic nature trails. Florida's parks, combined with wonderful weather, offer year-round fun for all ages. Events such as battle reenactments and Native American festivals celebrate Florida's past, while art shows, museums and lighthouses offer a look into Florida's cultural heritage.

For more information on Florida's park system and a comprehensive list or parks visit:

floridastateparks.org

Lighthouses

People are continually enchanted by the history, lore, and romance embodied by lighthouses. Visiting and learning about lighthouses has become a passion for people of all ages. Being that it's nearly surrounded by water, Florida has a large number of lighthouses. Many are open to the public for tours, and some are even available to climb.

According to the Florida Lighthouse Association, there are 29 remaining historic lighthouses in Florida. Some of these are among the nation's oldest and tallest, such as Ponce de Leon Inlet Lighthouse (2nd tallest in U.S.), the only Florida lighthouse registered as a national landmark. The Florida Lighthouse Association, whose mission is to preserve Florida's remaining lights, offers some great information on the history of lighthouses in Florida at the website:

floridalighthouses.org

Fishing and Boating

Not many places in the world, let alone in the United States, can beat Florida when it comes to the quality of fishing and boating. In fact, with 7,700 lakes, 10,550 miles of rivers, and 2,276 miles of tidal shoreline, Florida is the "fishing capital of the world" and some would consider it the boating capital of the world also. Florida has a large variety of species of fish, from largemouth bass in the fresh waters, to redfish along the shoreline to sailfish offshore. More anglers come to Florida to fish than anywhere else in the nation.

Florida has the highest number of registered recreational boats in the nation. And why wouldn't it, with water every-where you turn? Boating is a favorite recreational pastime of many Floridians and visitors to the state and an excellent way to relax and spend time with friends and family. No matter where you are in Florida: North, South, East or West, inland or on the coast, good fishing and boating are just outside your door.

For more information on fishing and boating in Florida, as well as license information for both, visit:

visitflorida.com/things-to-do/fishing/

myfwc.com/boating/

CHAPTER TWENTY-EIGHT
CONTINUE THE JOURNEY

CONGRATULATIONS! You've made it to the end of this guide to Florida retirement. But there's no need to stop now!

First off, if you enjoyed this book I'd be grateful if you left a positive review for me on Amazon or wherever you bought it. Every little bit helps get the word out!

If you'd like to connect with me and continue learning more about retirement in Florida, I've created a way for you to do just that.

Florida Retirement Insider is a private, member's only online community where you can get access to exclusive content, community tours, video courses, connect with other future Florida retirees, and more.

Florida Retirement Insider makes it easy to connect with and learn from others on the same path to retirement in Florida as you.

How much time, energy, and effort will you save by learning from others going through the same things as you are?

You can learn more and join here:

floridaforboomers.com/insider

Made in the USA
Columbia, SC
05 June 2023

17673138R00163